'Robert Inchausti is a lifelong scholar and teacher of the luminous and mystical as it appears in the soul and in the streets. In *The Way of Thomas Merton*, he continues to illuminate the journey of the contemplative to "seek the centre of his own living truth", as Merton himself described. This is the unavoidable odyssey of the modern soul: to find our enduring kinship through our irrevocable authenticity. Inchausti models this while weaving countless insights from the ages.'
Mark Nepo, poet, philosopher and author of *Surviving Storms*

'In his insightful illumination of Thomas Merton's journey, Inchausti provides fuel for our search for the authentic self that lies beneath our everyday yearnings. To read this book is to re-engage with the most important questions of our lives. While no one can take your journey for you, Inchausti's poetically insightful reflection on Thomas Merton's life of deep inquiry opens a window through which you may discover your own unique pathway home.'
Ward Mailliard, co-founder of the Mount Madonna Center, Watsonville, California

'This Lenten devotional is unlike any I've seen. It's not about giving up something trivial for a few weeks. It's about getting free of the "false self" that alienates us from ourselves, one another and God. Nobody understood that transformation better than Thomas Merton – and nobody understands Merton better than Robert Inchausti, whose spiritual sensibilities run deep and true. As a long-time Merton student and fellow seeker, I learned much from this brilliant treatise. I believe you will, too.'
Parker J. Palmer, writer, speaker and author of *On the Brink of Everything*

Robert Inchausti is Emeritus Professor of English at California State Polytechnic University in San Luis Obispo, USA. He has written three books on Thomas Merton, most notably *Thomas Merton's American Prophecy*, and edited two volumes of Merton's writings, *The Pocket Thomas Merton* and *Echoing Silence: Thomas Merton on the Vocation of Writing*. Professor Inchausti's first book, *The Ignorant Perfection of Ordinary People*, was nominated for a National Book Award. His *Subversive Orthodoxy: Outlaws, Revolutionaries, and other Christians in Disguise* has recently been translated into Portuguese and published in Brazil. His years teaching English at Christian Brothers High School under the mentorship of the controversial teacher/mystic "Brother Blake" are chronicled in Inchausti's memoir *Spitwad Sutras: Classroom Teaching as Sublime Vocation* – which is still taught in teacher-education courses across the USA. Robert lives on the Central of California with his wife Linda Garcia-Inchausti and two dogs Pancho and Besito.

THE WAY OF THOMAS MERTON

A prayer journey through Lent

Robert Inchausti

First published in Great Britain in 2022

Society for Promoting Christian Knowledge
36 Causton Street
London SW1P 4ST
www.spck.org.uk

British Library Cataloguing-in-Publication Data
A catalogue record for this book is available from the British Library

ISBN 978–0–281–08582–8
eBook ISBN 978–0–281–08609–2

1 3 5 7 9 10 8 6 4 2

Typeset by Falcon Oast Graphic Art Ltd
First printed in Great Britain by Clays Ltd

eBook by Falcon Oast Graphic Art Ltd

Produced on paper from sustainable sources

'The contemplative does not set out to achieve a kind of intuitive mastery of history, or of man's spirit, or of the things of God. He seeks the center of his own living truth, and there all he needs to perceive of these other mysteries is granted to him at the moment when he needs it. If he needs nothing, nothing is granted. And if nothing is granted, then nothing is desired. The wisdom of the contemplative is then, not the wisdom of a man who needs to possess knowledge and learning (though he may be a learned man). It is the wisdom of a man who has forgotten himself and forgotten wisdom, and who seeks to possess nothing because he needs nothing. All that he needs comes to him from God, even before he begins to need it.'
Thomas Merton (*The Inner Experience*)

Contents

Abbreviations

The following abbreviations have been used to refer to works by Thomas Merton. Publication details can be found in 'Works cited' at the end of the book.

AJ	*The Asian Journal of Thomas Merton*
CFT	*The Courage for Truth*
CGB	*Conjectures of a Guilty Bystander*
CIWA	*Contemplation in a World of Action*
CMP	*The Climate of Monastic Prayer*
CQR	*Cistercian Quarterly Review*
CP	*Contemplative Prayer*
DQ	*Disputed Questions*
FAV	*Faith and Violence*
HGL	*The Hidden Ground of Love*
HR	*Honorable Reader*
IE	*The Inner Experience*
LB	*Living Bread*
LE	*The Literary Essays of Thomas Merton*
LL	*Love and Living*
MA	*My Argument with the Gestapo*
MR	*A Thomas Merton Reader*
NM	*No Man is an Island*
NS	*New Seeds of Contemplation*
OTB	*Opening the Bible*
PTM	*The Pocket Thomas Merton*
RJ	*Road to Joy* (with Robert Daggy)
RU	*Raids on the Unspeakable*
SD	*Seeds of Destruction*
SJ	*The Secular Journal of Thomas Merton*

List of abbreviations

SOC	*The School of Charity*
SOJ	*The Sign of Jonas*
SS	*A Search for Solitude*
SSM	*The Seven Storey Mountain*
TIS	*Thoughts in Solitude*
TL	'Time and Liturgy'
WOD	*Wisdom of the Desert*
Z&B	*Zen and the Birds of Appetite*

Introduction

Let's begin with a parable.

In the 1980s – before the fall of the USSR – the Czechoslovakian playwright Vaclav Havel found himself in prison for criticizing the puppet Communist regime then ruling his country. When the regime fell and democratic elections were held, he was unexpectedly elected the first president of the newly formed Czech-Slovak Republic, while he was still in prison!

When he was finally released and took office, he was hit by an attack of self-doubt and 'writer's block'. He had known what to say as a critic of the regime, but he had no idea what to say as its President. As a result, he fell into a deep and persistent depression.

Several years later, Havel wrote a play about this transitional period in his life, titled *Largo Desolato*. In one of its key scenes (and I am speaking now from memory based on a production I saw many years ago), Havel's protagonist is lamenting to his literary agent that he does not know who he is any more and that he hasn't anything left to say. Then the doorbell rings, and standing before him is a young college student, one of his fans.

She tells him that she recently finished reading his book *The Phenomenology of Love* while riding home on the bus, and when she looked up from her reading, everyone around her seemed to be glowing. She wanted to tell them they were all shining like stars, but she didn't know what to say. So she made a promise to herself that she would seek out the author and ask him, 'How do you do it? How do you tell people that they are all radiant like angels?'

Havel replies,

You have just given me the greatest compliment any reader can give to a writer. You have asked me to explain to you the meaning of life. But the meaning of life is not like an answer to a question you hear once and remember for the rest of your life. It is more like a house that you live in. Unfortunately, I don't live in that house any longer. But I can tell by your question that you do. So why don't you come in, and we can talk, and maybe you can show me the way back to the house of meaning.

Thomas Merton's writing often evokes the same kind of invitation to his readers. They feel he has somehow ushered them back into their own house of meaning, that his words seem written specifically for them and, somehow, even partially *by them* – and that their participation *as readers* is required in filling out the truth of what he has to say.

Unlike other so-called 'spiritual masters', Merton doesn't have an answer to all of life's most vexing questions. Like Vaclav Havel, indeed like most of us, he moves in and out of the 'house of meaning' all the time.

If you are not familiar with the life and works of Thomas Merton, then you may be surprised, if not scandalized, by the story about to unfold here. For as this book's epigraph informs you, Thomas Merton, the bestselling author and renowned Catholic contemplative, did not aspire to a mastery of history nor of human nature, nor even of 'the things of God'. 'Such knowledge', he tells us, 'if it is to be of any real use, only emerges as needed from the center of our own living truth.'

Merton's aim was to live from the centre of his own living truth, like a child or bird of the field, secure in the knowledge that God will provide what is needed even before we know what it is that we need.

Rowan Williams, the former Archbishop of Canterbury, explained Merton's unique significance this way:

Being interested in Merton is not being interested in an original, or 'shaping mind', but being interested in God and human possibilities. Merton will not let us look at him for long: he will, finally, persuade us to look in the direction he is looking.[1]

And Merton is looking in the direction of God – 'the one who lives and speaks in us both'. As a result, the subject of any book by, on, or about Thomas Merton is really about who we are in relationship to God. The problem is, as Merton takes such great pains to explain, God is too often hidden from us under a fog of worldly cares and abstract conceptions that keep us living in confusion as to who we are and what truly matters.

Merton called this stubborn, coveting, self-centred aspect of our lives 'the false self' and described its dynamics in this way:

> The deep secrecy of my own being is often hidden from me by my own estimate of what I am. My idea of what I am is falsified by my admiration for what I do. And my illusions about myself are bred by contagion from the illusions of other men. We all seek to imitate one another's imagined greatness. If I do not know who I am, it is because I think I am the sort of person everyone around me wants to be. Perhaps I have never asked myself whether I really want to become what everyone else seems to want to become. Perhaps if I only realized that I do not admire what everyone else seems to admire, I would really begin to live after all. I would be liberated from the painful duty of saying what I really do not think and acting in a way that betrays God's truth and the integrity of my own soul.
> (*NM*, pp. 125–6)

The very first page of his internationally bestselling autobiography *The Seven Storey Mountain* (1948) begins with a similar confession:

> I came into the world free by nature, in the image of God. I was, nevertheless, the prisoner of my own violence and my own selfishness, in the image of the world into which I was born; that world was the picture of Hell, full of men like myself, loving God, and yet hating him; born to love him, living instead in fear and hopeless self-contradictory hungers.
> (*SSM*, p. 3)

Pope Francis quoted these lines in his address to a joint session of the United States Congress in 2015 because they highlighted one of the great themes of his pontificate: our need for mercy. Although Merton later took back his description of the world as 'the picture of Hell', dismissing it as the hyperbole of the recently converted; given that Merton was born in 1915 in France, not very far from the killing fields of the First World War, in retrospect this description doesn't seem hyperbolic at all.

The problem, Merton is pointing out here, isn't just that we tell ourselves lies but that we *live* them. All around us in the culture and deep within our minds and bodily memories reside deceits, exaggerations and half-truths that wreak havoc with our emotional and spiritual well-being, distorting our relationship to God, ourselves and others.

I think it is fair to say that in all his journals, letters and autobiographical works Merton wrote primarily to 'unlie' the falsehoods that he was born into and consequently lived by. Writing opened a way for him to discover his own 'true self'.

The true and false self are tricky terms because the 'false self' as Merton uses the term is not 'bad' nor is it exactly 'false'. It is, perhaps, more correctly understood as imitative and conditioned. It is our identity as a self-conscious social being given us by the culture we are born into – not our divine reality in relation to the Absolute.

To borrow a term from the philosophical anthropologist René Girard, our false self is our *mimetic self* – the socio-political part of our minds made up of what we say about ourselves, as well as anything anyone else says about us. It is, in other words, an image in our heads, a phantasmagoria.

By contrast, our 'true self' is not really a 'self' at all. It is consciousness or, if you prefer, Christ consciousness: being one with God, which is also to say one with the Holy Spirit and, so also, one with everyone else (Colossians 3.3).

Merton explained the difference between the 'true self' and the 'false self':

The 'I' that works in the world, thinks about itself, observes its own reactions and talks about itself is not the true 'I' that has

been united to God in Christ . . . Contemplation is precisely the awareness that this 'I' is really 'not I' and the awakening of the unknown 'I' that is beyond observation and reflection and is incapable of commenting upon itself.
(*NS*, p. 7; see 1 John 3.2)

Given this asymmetrical inner divide, how can any writer over-come their own 'false self' to communicate directly to readers, 'true self to true self'? Is such a thing even possible? Merton explained his aspirations as a writer:

It is not as an author that I would speak to you, not as a story-teller, not as a philosopher, not as a friend only: I seek to speak to you, in some way, as your own self. Who can tell what this may mean? I myself do not know. But if you listen, things will be said that are perhaps not written in this book. And this will be due not to me, but to the One who lives and speaks in both.
(*HR*, p. 67; see Galatians 2.20)

Towards the end of *Seeds of Contemplation* (1948) (the book that signalled Merton's permanent move away from the idiom of neo-scholasticism to the examination of his own personal faith experiences), Merton explained the reader's role in such an exchange:

The purpose of a book of meditations is to teach you how to think and not to do your thinking for you. Consequently, if you pick up such a book and simply read through it you are wasting your time. As soon as any thought stimulates your mind or your heart you can put the book down because your meditation has begun.

To think that you are somehow obliged to follow the author of the book to his own particular conclusion would be a great mistake. It may happen that his conclusion does not apply to you. God may want you to end up somewhere else. He may

have planned for you quite a different grace than the one the author suggests you might be needing.
(*NS*, p. 215)

The soul-work of reading, it turns out, is quite similar to the soul-work of writing. Both point to a third, yet often unperceived, participant – the Holy Spirit. But in order for this Trinitarian communion to take place, both writer and reader must allow themselves to be addressed, and this is not something anyone can force upon the other. It is a grace that falls upon the open-hearted like rain (or fatigue).

This book won't focus on Merton's literary style (he had many of them). Nor will it pore over the finer points of his theology (he was an orthodox Catholic his entire adult life). Instead, the focus will be on his 'center of living truth' as an aid in helping us to find our own.

Let this book be your invitation to do just that.

We will look closely at key passages from Merton's journals, poetry, letters, essays and memoirs, encouraged by the words of Flavian Burns – Merton's last abbot – who said in an interview not long after Merton's death, 'While I'm very happy that I did know him, I always felt the deeper part of Merton he revealed only in his books.'[2]

A personal note

When I was a college student, I met an inspirational English professor who was a lot like Merton's mentor Mark Van Doren. His classes spoke to a part of me I had not previously known existed, and this set me on a path of contemplative reading and self-inquiry that has lasted to this day.

But back then I wanted this professor to know how deeply his lectures had affected me, so I went to his office hour one day to tell him. Of course, the whole conversation was terribly awkward.

He asked me if I liked his class, and when I said 'Yes', he asked me 'Why?'

I told him I had learned more about myself in just one of his lectures on Franz Kafka than I had learned in three years of high school.

'What did you learn?'

I could tell by the way he asked the question that he wasn't just asking about what I remembered from his lecture but rather what that lecture had done to me as a human being – about what it had taught me about life.

It was a *real question* that deserved a *real answer*.

'I guess the main thing that I learned', I said, 'is that I'm a complete idiot.'

When I looked away in embarrassment, he said, 'Don't feel bad. This country manufactures idiots. There's no way you could have escaped it.'

'But what do I do now? How do I stop being an idiot?'

'Just stop being an idiot!' he said. As if the idiot I had made of myself could just as easily be unmade by myself. Up to this point in my life I had just not yet received a compelling enough invitation to do it.

What follows in this book are the compelling invitations and subsequent 'unmakings' that transformed Thomas Merton from – in the words of his fellow monk Matthew Kelty – 'an ignorant pagan, rich and spoiled' into someone Pope Francis has described as one of the four greatest prophetic figures in American history, equal in stature to Abraham Lincoln, Martin Luther King and Dorothy Day. Along the way we will pause to consider our own relationship to this unfolding story in terms of its significance to our own ultimate concerns.

Questions for reflection and discussion

1 Is there an invitation you are waiting to receive that has not yet arrived in your life? What are you waiting for?
2 How valuable an experience are you planning this book to be for you?
3 How do you experience God in your life?
4 What is the title of the story of the part of your life that is just now coming to an end? What is the title of the new story that is just beginning?

1

An apostle, not a genius

Life is an experimental journey undertaken involuntarily. It is a journey of the spirit through the material world and, since it is the spirit that travels, it is the spirit that is experienced. That is why there exist contemplative souls who have lived more intensely, more widely, more tumultuously than others who have lived their lives purely externally.
(Fernando Pessoa, *The Book of Disquiet*)

Prophecy and contemplation seem, at first, to be two very different callings, one public, the other private. Prophecy considers contemporary events in the light of their inherent, internal contradictions straining towards the future. Contemplation considers the movement of grace in individual lives. To speak of a 'prophetic contemplative' is to speak of a hybrid charism largely pioneered in our time by the writer/monk Thomas Merton whose life was lived, as he put it, 'within the belly of a paradox' (*SOJ*, frontispiece).

This is an understatement to be sure, for Thomas Merton was a man of many contradictions: a mystic who advocated social change, a poet who believed silence was the ultimate eloquence, a social critic who distrusted sociological categories, and a world-famous hermit. These paradoxes do not resolve themselves easily; indeed, they don't resolve themselves at all but rather point to a distinction Søren Kierkegaard once made between the genius and the apostle.

The genius, Kierkegaard wrote, has 'only an immanent teleology' while the apostle is 'absolutely, paradoxically teleologically placed'.[1] Genius, in other words, is the fulfilment of a human potentiality and expresses itself in works that are ends in themselves: master-pieces that come to define what our culture takes to be a 'classic' – that is to say, a true and definitive representation of the human condition.

On the other hand, apostles are not geniuses. They exist in a paradoxical relationship to the human enterprise as an end in itself. For them, culture – even in its highest forms of expression – is always a bit limited.

Apostles point beyond achievement, beyond history, beyond even life itself to some as yet unimaginable messianic end, some mystery God prefers not yet to disclose. Apostles are absolute dissidents and metaphysical rebels whose primary contribution to everyday life is to expose its falsities and deceits by drowning them in the light of a higher revelation.

Thomas Merton was an apostle, not a genius. He did not write timeless works of poetry or masterpieces of theology. He was a different kind of writer altogether. Pope Francis described him as 'a man of prayer, a thinker who challenged the certitudes of his time and opened new horizons for souls and for the Church'. That is to say, Merton exposed the half-truths his countrymen, his Church (and even he himself) had settled for.

He questioned easy answers and rote responses, preferring ineffable experience to articulated doctrine, Zen koans[2] to philosophical positivism, dissent to complacency, heartbreak over arrogance, and the *via negativa* to systematic theology. He never intended his ideas to be translated into doctrine or codified into laws, regulations or schools of prayer. In fact, the very idea of 'Mertonism' made him shudder.

In a 1963 personal letter to one of his fellow monks, Father Chrysogonis Waddell, Merton protested:

> If there is such a thing as 'Mertonism,' I suppose I am the one that ought to be aware of it. The people who believe in this term evidently do not know how unwilling I would be to have anyone repeat in his own life the miseries of mine. That would be flatly a mortal sin against charity . . . anyone who imitates me does so at his own risk. I can promise him some fine moments of naked despair.
> (*SOC*, p. 186)

Aa a Christian apostle, Merton's desire – to let God speak through him – was always greater than his own capacity to fulfil it, and his audience never merely mortal. Like most serious writers, Merton knew he was only 'sometimes' a genius, but he was *always an apostle* – which put him at odds with both kitsch Catholicism and the techno-corporate idols of his age.

In fact, Merton often explicitly instructed his readers to turn away from the ideas on the page to attend to their own inner silence and solitude, to stop thinking about how he might have suggested they ought to live and begin living themselves.

What is exemplary about Merton is not his moral perfection nor his piety nor even his self-awareness as to his own failures and hypocrisies, but rather the candour and exactitude with which he articulates the lessons of 'mistakes owned' and 'deceits un-lied'. His life was no pilgrim's progress to perfection, but a series of turnabouts, mortifications and crises, accompanied by an equal number of graces, recognition scenes and self-corrections.

He admits as much in the following passage from *Raids on the Unspeakable*, which could very well serve as the preface to the book you are now reading.

> If I dare, in these few words, to ask you some direct and personal questions, it is because I address them as much to myself as to you. It is because I am still able to hope that a civil exchange of ideas can take place between two persons – that we have not yet reached the stage where we are all hermetically sealed, each one in the collective ignorance and despair of his [or her] own herd. If I seem to be in a hurry to take advantage of the situation that still exists, it is frankly, because I sometimes feel it may not continue to exist much longer. In any case, I believe that we are still sufficiently 'persons' to realize we have a common difficulty and try to solve it together.
> (*RU*, p. 54)

Questions for reflection and discussion

1 If God does not want perfection from us, what *does* God want from us?

2 What do others assume about you – based on your voice, opinions or appearance – that you wished they wouldn't assume?

3 Have you ever misread another person's character because you assumed that person fits a stereotype you yourself unconsciously held about them? What was this self-discovery like?

2

The *via negativa*

This is the ultimate in human knowledge of God: to know that
we do not know Him.

(Thomas Aquinas, *Questiones Disputatiae de Potentia Dei*)

Catholic tradition recognizes two different – yet complementary –
approaches to Christian spirituality – both defined by Pseudo-
Dionysius, the fifth-century monastic writer. Kataphatic or 'positive'
spirituality sees God in all things; whereas, apophatic or 'negative' spirituality seeks to experience God directly through prayerful
attention to the ineffable Absolute.

Merton's way is the way of unknowing – the *via negativa*
(apophatic spirituality) – which requires the unknowing of who we
think we are in order to become who God created us to be. This is
a paradoxical 'achievement' because it really isn't an achievement at
all but the act of letting go of our limited concepts of God and ourselves in order to enter the dark light of unknowing which unites us
with an inconceivable and ineffable God.

Merton tells us:

All sin starts from the assumption that my false self, the self
that exists only in my own egocentric desires, is the fundamental reality of life to which everything else in the universe
is ordered. Thus, I use up my life in the desire for pleasures
and the thirst for experiences, for power, honour, knowledge, and love to clothe this false self and construct its
nothingness into something objectively real. And I wind
experiences around myself and cover myself with pleasures
and glory like bandages in order to make myself perceptible
to myself and the world, as if I were an invisible body that

could only become visible when something visible covered its
surface.
(*NS*, pp. 34–5)

So, when Merton says that 'We all seek to imitate one another's
imagined greatness', he is saying that the source of our greed and
violence resides in our envy of others. But more than that, he is
offering us the *via negativa* as the antidote to envy. 'If we just asked
ourselves', he says, 'whether we really wanted to become what
everyone else seems to want to become, we might break the trance
that blinds us – and begin to see things through the divine dark light
of our own true selves' (*NM*, pp. 125–6) (Luke 17.21; Psalm 46.10).

The problem is that our 'false self' wants us to 'be somebody' – 'a
presence', 'a persona', somebody 'better' or 'more famous' than who
we are. It scans the world for models of what to want and how to be,
forfeiting the radical originality of just being ourselves.

The Franciscan Richard Rohr put it this way: 'You do not climb
up to your True Self. You fall into it, so don't avoid all falling. There,
ironically and happily, you are finally found.'[1]

Merton's version of this truism is less pithy but a bit more detailed:

The real 'I' is just simply ourselves and nothing more. Nothing
more, nothing less. Our self as we are in the eyes of God, to
use Christian terms. Our self in all our uniqueness, dignity, lit-
tleness, and ineffable greatness: the greatness we have received
from God our Father and that we share with Him because
He is our Father and 'In Him we live and move and have
our being.'
(*IE*, p. 11; see Acts 17.28)

Just as Augustine prayed, 'Grant, Lord, that I may know myself that
I may know thee', Merton – Augustine's twentieth-century mirror
image – reverses the terms: 'Grant, Lord, that I may know thee so
that I may know myself.'

And yet the false self is not really a 'bad' self. It is just our 'survival' or 'mimetic' self.

As children we mimic the values, attitudes and language of the adults around us so we that can survive our upbringings. Each of us is born into a specific family mythology and socio-historical context that shapes who-we-believe-we-are, based on the opinions and examples of others (Luke 17.33).

The poet William Wordsworth famously described it this way:

Not in entire forgetfulness,
    And not in utter nakedness,
But trailing clouds of glory do we come
    From God who is our home . . .
Shades of the prison-house begin to close
    Upon the growing Boy . . .
At length the Man perceives it die away,
And fade into the light of common day.[2]

As time passes, the once visionary pre-schooler acquires what Merton calls the 'I' of individuality. This 'I' of individuality or 'false self' is only 'false' in the sense that it trades in the infinite potential of our likeness to God for the conventional 'somebody' we must become in order to navigate the various worlds of our everyday existence.

We make our conditioned identities 'real' by suppressing our awareness of their radical contingency and spiritual poverty just to *get by* and *fit in*. It then takes a turning away from the false self to the second innocence of our 'true self' to complete our spiritual journey back to God who is our home (*RU*, pp. 15–16).

One of Merton's favourite poets, the Portuguese writer Fernando Pessoa, described it this way:

We all have two lives: The true, the one we dreamed of in childhood and go on dreaming of as adults in a substratum of mist; and the false, the one we love when we live with others, the practical, the useful, the one that ends up being put in a coffin.[3]

By explicating this distinction, Merton wasn't saying anything new, but he was placing contemporary alienation within a contemplative

14

spiritual tradition many centuries old, a tradition that had been downplayed ever since the Enlightenment when our interiorly divided 'fallen' selves were replaced by a single, rational, autonomous, modern 'self' – the Cartesian cogito.

One of Merton's prayers calls attention to this blunder and to the difficult moral challenges we face as moderns holding a view of ourselves as rational creatures when we are more truly inwardly divided 'Promethean tyros' enamoured by a false sense of superiority over the entirety of God's creation. Here's the prayer:

> Teach me to bear a humility which shows me without ceasing, that I am a liar and a fraud and that, even though this is so, I have an obligation to strive after truth, to be as true as I can, even though I will inevitably find all my truth half poisoned with deceit. This is the terrible thing about humility: that it is never fully successful. If it were only possible to be completely humble on this earth. But no, that's the trouble. You, Lord, were humble. But our humility consists in being proud and knowing all about it, and being cursed by the unbearable weight of it, and to be able to do so little about it.
> (*TIS*, pp. 59–60)

The good news here is that no matter who we pretend to be or what it is we think we desire, our true selves remain within us hidden with Christ in God (Matthew 18.1–6; Mark 10.13–16). They might only reveal themselves to us in dreams, wordless intuitions or fleetingly unexpected pangs of conscience, but no matter how hard we may try to ignore them, their call urges us again and again to 'Be ourselves' – that all that we want, think, feel and believe is not really us. For our true selves do not just lie within us, but immeasurably high above us, beyond our egos and even beyond what we may think of as our desires – 'absolutely, paradoxically, teleologically placed'.

Merton tells us:

> We have the choice, between the external mask which seems to be real and which lives by the shadowy autonomy for the brief

moment of earthly existence, and the hidden, inner person who seems to us to be nothing, but who can give themselves eternally to the truth in whom they subsist. It is this inner self that is taken up into the mystery of Christ, by His love, by the Holy Spirit, so that in secret we live in Christ.
(*NS*, p. xii; see Colossians 3.3; Galatians 2.20)

To do this, we must disengage from the stories we tell ourselves about ourselves (even the stories of our remarkable religiosity) in order to allow God to reveal his story of us to us in all its unexpected originality, freshness and challenge. The Christian virtues of humility, compunction, prayer, stillness, introspection, solitude and confession are all ways of stepping back from our socially constructed 'heroic' selves so that we might enter into the stillness, silence, solitude, grace and childlike originality of who we really are. As Merton says:

True solitude is selfless. Therefore, it is rich in silence and charity and peace. It finds in itself seemingly inexhaustible resources of good to bestow on other people. False solitude is self-centered. And because it finds nothing in its own center, it seeks to draw all things into itself. But everything it touches becomes infected with its own nothingness, and falls apart.
(*PTM*, p. xi)

In *Conjectures of a Guilty Bystander*, Merton put it this way: 'At the center of our being is a point of nothingness which is untouched by sin and by illusion, a point of pure truth, a point or spark which belongs entirely to God' (*CGB*, p. 158).

But, there is an even better formulation of the true self in *Zen and the Birds of Appetite*, published in 1968:

The (True) Self is not its own centre and does not orbit around itself; it is centred on God, the one centre of all, which is 'everywhere and nowhere.' In whom all are encountered, from whom all proceed. Thus, from the very start this consciousness

is disposed to encounter 'the other' with whom it is already
united anyway 'in God.'
(*Z&B*, p. 24)

Our true selves recognize the contingency of our existence, our
impermanence and our radical need; whereas, our false self plays
a part, adopts a role, and enters into social dramas that provide the
illusion of individuality, autonomy, and independence. Our false
self is the person we think we are or pretend to be – our social
media self – a creature made of postures and flattering selfies that
mimic those of movie stars and social media influencers. It's the self
we pretend to be or believe we could be if circumstances had only
fallen our way. It is a myth we tell ourselves about ourselves, but it
is nobody God knows. It isn't real.

Questions for reflection and discussion

1 Does Merton's distinction between the true and false self make
  sense to you? Why or why not?
2 Have you ever felt yourself inhabited by a false self? A part of
  you that wants to go on talking when you know you should stop
  and listen? Or a part of you that wants to stay angry when your
  heart knows you are already over it? What do these experiences
  tell you about your 'true self', if anything?
3 If you prefer not to reflect or discuss these questions, what
  story are you telling yourself about why you are refusing this
  invitation?

3

Finding our true selves

For me, to be a saint means to be myself.
(Thomas Merton, *NS*)

The Girardian scholar James Alison (author of *The Joy of Being Wrong*) finds a connection between Merton's idea of the false self and what the social theorist René Girard calls 'mimetic desire', the psychological mechanism through which human beings unconsciously decide for themselves who they want to be through their imitation of exemplary others – models and idols whose being (and power) they want for themselves.[1]

Alison explains his version of the *via negativa* this way:

I take it that contemplation is a certain sort of seeing.

I take it from Girard that we always learn to see through the eyes of another.

The desire of another directs our seeing and makes available to us what is to be seen.

I also take it that when we talk about contemplation in a Christian context, we are talking about quite a specific sort of seeing. We are talking about learning how to be given our desire through the eyes of another. The other is Jesus, the Word of God. So, we are being taught to look at *what is* through the eyes of the One who reveals the mind of God. That is, to be possessed by the mind of God ourselves.

By being taught to receive ourselves and all that is around us through the eye and desire of God, our 'self' becomes an incarnation of that desire, and we start to speak words formed by the un-hypnosis, the awakening desire of the Creator. In other words: we are being taught to be loving lookers at *what is* by the One who is calling into being and loving *what is*. We are being taught to see and delight in *what is* by the One whose delighting is what gives it, and us, to be.[2]

Alison's description of Christian contemplation as 'un-hypnosis' (or 'anti-mimesis') helps to explain why there is no official Mertonian school of mystical prayer nor patented Merton meditation protocols and why Merton himself went to such great lengths to discourage the formation of any clubs or cults based on his personal devotional practices.

Merton clearly never wanted to hypnotize anyone; quite the contrary, he wanted to free himself and us from any servile subjection to the 'false self' born of mimetic desire. For Merton, no one need imitate his (or anyone else's) way of thinking or praying because each one of us is called by God to become our own version of Christ through the gift of the Holy Spirit (Galatians 2.22).

There are many names for the persons we think we are or want to be – the false self, *persona*, ego, Cartesian cogito, the 'I' of individuality, and so on. But there is really no name for our 'true self' because it is simply who we are when we are not busy 'being' somebody else. Our 'true self', in other words, is the spirit of our being – our limitless interior life – unencumbered by any social rivalries or mediated desires (Matthew 10.39).

This is why, Merton advises us,

we should not look for a 'method' or 'system' by which to live our lives but, rather, cultivate the 'attitude' and 'outlook' of the beatitudes of faith (openness, attention, reverence, expectation, supplication, trust and joy). These virtues remind us that 'we are in the presence of God, that we live in Christ, that in the spirit of God we "see" God our Father without "seeing." We know him in "unknowing."'
(*CP*, p. 34)

In other words:

God's 'will' is not a force that presses down on us from the outside. It works from within us from the ontological core of our own freedom (our own living truth as human beings created in the image of God). Made free, in the image of God, our freedom contains in itself a demand for infinite freedom which can be met only by perfect union with the freedom of God, not only as an external norm, but as the source of our own love. Here philosophical notions of freedom necessarily break down and the perfect freedom of the Christian can be accounted for only by the indwelling Holy Spirit.
(*CGB*, p. 329)

The closest Merton ever came to revealing his own personal prayer practices surfaced in a private letter he wrote to Abdul Aziz, a Sufi professor living in Pakistan:

There is in my heart this great thirst to recognize totally all the nothingness of that which is not from God. My prayer then is a kind of praise rising up out of the centre of Nothingness and Silence. If I am still present 'myself,' this I recognize as an obstacle about which I can do nothing unless He himself removes the obstacle. Such is my ordinary way of prayer or meditation. It is not 'thinking about' anything *but a direct seeking of the Face of the Invisible.* I do not ordinarily write about such things, and I ask you to be discreet about it. But I write this as a testimony of confidence and friendship.
(*HGL*, p. 64; italics mine)

Merton found parallels to his own attempt to see 'the face of the invisible' in those provocative questions posed by Zen masters known as koans (for example, 'What face did you have before your mother was born?'). Those deftly crafted enigmas were designed to provoke in students a new state of consciousness by demonstrating that some things simply cannot be understood rationally. Access to some other dimension of experience is required for us to realize that we are already free and that the only thing we need is to become who we already are.

Koans express – in a Buddhist idiom – Merton's own Augustinian realization that 'God gave us a soul that was not made to bring itself to perfection in its own order, but to be perfected by Him in an order infinitely beyond the reach of human powers' (*SSM*, p. 185). The task, as Merton puts it, is to 'understand more and more the paradoxes in which you must live' (*SOC*, p. 355). 'This would be a depressing thought,' Merton says, 'were it not merely abstract. Because in the concrete order of things God gave man a nature that was ordered to a supernatural life' (*SSM*, p. 185).

Zen, like 'apophatic' Christianity, communicates an existential vision of the way things *are* by directly awakening us from the abstract concepts and memes we all too often substitute for concrete reality (or, more simply said, the 'maps' we mistake for the 'territory').

Consider these Christian 'koans' taken at random from Merton's private letters. Each provokes the reader to seek 'the hidden face of God': 'Christ did not die on the Cross merely so there might be devout Christians' (*CFT*, p. 77). And, perhaps just as challenging:

> I cannot be a Catholic unless it is made clear to the world that I am a Jew and a Moslem. Unless I am execrated as a Buddhist and denounced for having undermined all that this comfortable and social Catholicism stands for: this lining up of cassocks, this regimenting of birettas.
> (*CFT*, p. 79)

To understand what is being said here we must question what it commonly means to be a Christian.

In his Preface to *A Thomas Merton Reader*, Merton explains why he found the *via negativa* so central to his writing as well as to his own personal spiritual growth.

> I have tried to learn in my writing a monastic lesson I probably could not have learned otherwise: to let go of my idea of myself, to take myself with more than one grain of salt. If the monastic life is a life of hardship and sacrifice, I would say that for me most of the hardship has come in connection with

writing. It is possible to doubt whether I have become a monk (a doubt I have to live with), but it is not possible to doubt that I am a writer, that I was born one and will probably die as one. Disconcerting, dis-edifying as it is, this seems to be my lot and my vocation. It is what God has given me in order that I might give it back to him. In religious terms, this is simply a matter of accepting life, and everything in life as a gift, and clinging to none of it, as far as you are able.
(*MR*, pp. 16–17)

When Merton tells us that he feels he is more clearly a writer than a monk, I think he is acknowledging the fact that his capacity for critical discernment and literary acumen exceed – as it must – his awareness of his own soul. And so, however skilled he might have become at expressing himself, it was as a monk, as a Christian and as a man that the angelic jury was still out and would remain so until the end of his life.

Writing, in this sense, had become both his gift and his cross – an expression of the humanity he brought *to* his Christian conversion into the contemplative life. Merton reflects:

All life tends to grow like this, in mystery inscaped with para-dox and contradiction, yet centered, in its very heart, on divine mercy. Such is my philosophy, and it is more than philosophy because it consists not in statements about a truth that cannot be adequately stated, but in grace, mercy, and the realization of the 'new life' that is in us who believe, by the gift of the Holy Spirit.
(*MR*, p. 17; see 2 Peter 1.4)

This is why 'the way to find the real "world"', Merton tells us,

is not merely to measure and observe what is outside us, but to discover our own inner ground. For that is where the world is, first of all: in my deepest self. This 'ground,' this 'world' where I am mysteriously present at once to my own self and to the freedoms of all other men, is not a visible, objective,

determined structure with fixed laws and demands. It is a living and self-creating mystery of which I am myself a part, to which I am myself my own unique door.
(*CIWA*, pp. 154–5)

It is by listening to our conscience, accepting our limitations and waiting in humble silence and solitude – attentive to God's grace and trusting in God's good time – that we can attain any purchase on our 'true selves' at all. Not by living up to the expectations of our parents, peers, school, colleagues, culture or even the Church – but by following the imperatives of our own true selves. 'Therefore,' Merton continues,

the problem of sanctity and salvation is, in fact, the problem of finding out who I am and of discovering my true self . . . We are at liberty to be real or to be unreal. We may be true or false, the choice is ours . . . But we cannot make these choices with impunity. Causes have effects and if we lie to ourselves and to others, then we cannot expect to find truth and reality whenever we happen to want them. If we have chosen the way of falsity, we must not be surprised that the truth eludes us when we finally come to need it.
(*NS*, pp. 31–2)

Questions for reflection and discussion

1 What has been given to you to give back to others (without worrying too much about how it might be received)?
2 When you pray, do you experience God from *within* or from *without*?
3 What is the 'no' (or refusal) that you keep postponing?
4 How can you get closer to who you *really are* as opposed to who you want to be?
5 Have you ever caught yourself leaving behind the 'I' of individualism? In that moment, who or what did you become?

4

The art of loss

Life is growth in the art of loss.
(John O'Donoghue, *Eternal Echoes*)

An editor who was putting together a book on 'successful Americans' once wrote to Merton and asked him to contribute his advice on 'how to become a successful writer'. Merton wrote back explaining that he had spent the better part of his life avoiding what is commonly thought of as 'success', that his bestseller was 'an accident due to inattention and naiveté', and that he was 'taking pains to make sure it would never happen again'.

If he had any message to those seeking success, he said, it would be this:

Be anything you like, be madmen, drunks, and bastards of every shape and form, but at all costs avoid one thing: success ... I believe I can thank Columbia University, among so many other things, for having helped me learn the value of unsuccess. Instead of preparing me for one of those splendid jobs on Madison Avenue, Columbia cured me forever of wanting one. Mark Van Doren and Joseph Wood Krutch taught me to imitate not Rockefeller but Thoreau ... Life does not have to be regarded as a game in which scores are kept and somebody wins. If you are too intent on winning, you will never enjoy playing. If you are too obsessed with success, you will forget how to live. If you have learned only how to be a success, your life has probably been wasted. If a university concentrates on producing successful people, it is lamentably failing in its obligation to society and to the students themselves.
(*LL*, p. 10; see Luke 18.14)

As you might have guessed, Merton's reply was never published. But he made his point: getting what you want is no guarantee of happiness. And seeing yourself as a 'success' turns you into a figment of your own imagination. Those who worship success never truly succeed because they do not fathom how bearing one's cross could be the very victory they seek. They have yet to get their minds around the basic, paradoxical Christian truism that to find oneself, one must lose oneself (John 12.24).

Kenosis is the term theologians use to describe this act of emptying so that God may fill us. Our life's purpose is not to surpass the achievements of our peers, not to become rich, nor is it even to fulfil our dreams or follow our bliss. It is, rather, to aspire to such worthy and transcendent goals that however often or repeatedly we may fail, we nevertheless fail gloriously in making the attempt (Philippians 2.5–8).

Great aspirations – if they are truly great – cannot be fulfilled. To speak the truth, to live in faith, to establish justice or to simply do no harm are never completely achieved. And so, many are tempted to sacrifice an authentic life in the service of great ideals for more attainable aims – like making a lot of money, obtaining material comfort or more power and more fame. And, for some of us, it's possible to get some of these things – if we live a self-centred enough life and look out for our own interests at every turn. But in our hearts, we know that living such an egocentric life hardly constitutes 'success' and that failing at a truly worthwhile end is far more satisfying and admirable (Luke 15.11–32).

The Irish Nobel Prize-winning author Samuel Beckett put it simply: 'No Matter, Try Again, Fail Again, Fail Better.'[1]

Merton elaborates:

A man who fails well is greater than one who succeeds badly. One who is content with what he has, and who accepts the fact that he inevitably misses very much in life, is far better off than one who has much but who worries about all that he may be missing. For we cannot make the best of what we are, if our hearts are always divided between what we are and what

25

we are not. The lower our estimate of ourselves and the lower our expectations, the greater chance we have of using what we have. If we do not know how poor we are, we will never be able to appreciate what we actually have.

But above all, we must learn our own weakness in order to awaken to a new order of action and of Being – *and experience God Himself accomplishing in us the things we find impossible.* We cannot be happy if we expect to live all the time at the highest peak of intensity. Happiness is not a matter of intensity but of balance and order and rhythm and harmony.
(*NM*, p. 127)

If we fail by the world's account, it may only mean that we have been spared the world's miscast aspirations. Tolstoy famously warned an ambitious Russian gentry addicted to progress and self-perfection that 'in an unequal unjust world run by a small minority – every so-called advance against nature and growth in efficiency is really a blow against human happiness and true social progress'. And so anyone who succeeds by attaining such short-sighted goals has quite literally failed by any reasonable measure, divine or human.

'The only true joy on earth', Merton tells us, 'is to escape from the prison of our own false self and enter by love into union with Life who dwells and sings within the essence of every creature and in the core of our souls' (*NS*, p. 25).

But what does this really mean?

Things become clearer when we consider Merton as 'an icon for brokenness'. James Finley called him that – not because Merton was any more broken than the rest of us, but because he embraced his weaknesses and flaws as an irreducible feature of the humanity he shared with everyone else. It was his acceptance of his limited, contingent, fallible self that made him an 'exceptional' person (if 'exceptional' is even the right word here).

'What we need', Merton writes,

is the gift of God which makes us able to find in ourselves, not just ourselves but Him, and then our nothingness becomes

26

His all. This is not possible without the liberation effected by compunction and humility. It requires not talent, not mere insight, but sorrow, pouring itself out in love and trust.
(*CQR*, p. 114; see Matthew 6.16)

Questions for reflection and discussion

1 How do you know you are following God in your life?
2 What are your thoughts as to who *you should be* at this moment in your life? Are these realistic expectations? Or someone else's expectations that you are applying to yourself?
3 Have you ever conjured up a false past or revved up feelings of nostalgia for things that never really happened? Those 'good old days' in middle school or your 'brilliant career' in junior football? Why do we misrepresent ourselves to ourselves?
4 From what depths in yourself are you answering these questions? Is there a deeper level you are holding back from?

5

The gifts of the wounded child

The Christian Maxim 'unless you become like little children, you shall not enter the kingdom of heaven' is my marker of the true self.
(Margaret Arden, *Midwifery of the Soul: A Holistic Perspective on Psychoanalysis*)

There is a saying attributed to the French novelist Gustave Flaubert that writers are people who find themselves born in a ditch and spend their lives trying to dig themselves out. That is to say, writers often don't know why they write, they write to find out. But the more they search, the further they get from any answer.

This ironic fate – true for many writers – was especially true for Thomas Merton.

His mother, an interior designer, died of stomach cancer when he was only 6 years old. A favourite aunt died when he was 8, and his peripatetic bohemian father – who painted watercolours in the spirit of Cézanne and took care of Tom as best he could while travelling to and from Europe – died of brain cancer when Tom was only 16 years old.

The psychotherapist Wayne Muller, author of *Legacy of the Heart: The Spiritual Advantages of a Painful Childhood*, describes the death of a parent early in life as 'a great storm' that rips through the family, and yet also 'a powerful meditation that pours a deluge of emotion and sensation into the lives of children'.

Hélène Cixous, in her book *Three Steps on the Ladder of Writing*, put the experience of a death in childhood as the first step on her 'ladder of writing'. Speaking of how the death of her father affected her as a child, she writes, 'His death gave me life from the beginning.'

The loss of a parent in childhood, she explains, feels like the end of the world, but it also opens up another world in its wake, and this other world is never quite what we expect it to be. The life on the far side of innocence is the beginning of *writing* which, for an artist, is also the beginning of *living*.

'Without that,' Cixous says, 'we know nothing about the mortality and immortality we carry. We don't know we're alive until we've encountered death.'[1]

It is not surprising that Merton harboured a sense of the fragility of existence and the tenuousness of human relationships from a very early age – later suffering panic attacks, bouts of severe depression and even contemplating suicide at least twice (that we know of).

Yet he also brought a precocious mixture of metaphysical longing and intellectual curiosity to his studies at school, attending a lonely lycée in France, then a slightly more gregarious Oakham public school in England (where he earned a reputation as a rebel) before his disastrous year at Clare College, Cambridge (more on this soon).

In retrospect, it seems that Merton's troubled adolescence was a part of what the psychotherapist Alice Miller called *The Drama of the Gifted Child*. She explains:

> When I used the word 'gifted' in the title, I had in mind neither children who receive high grades in school nor children talented in a special way. I simply meant all of us who have survived an abusive childhood thanks to an ability to adapt even to unspeakable cruelty [or loss] by becoming numb . . . Without this 'gift' offered us by nature, we would not have survived.[2]

Miller adds that mere survival is never enough, and it becomes the mission of many wounded children to win back for themselves the authority, guidance and security lost due to absent (or emotionally distant) caretakers. They often try to do this by winning admiration from their peers.

Of course, such vainglories never truly heal. Only by turning away from the 'public recognition' so cherished by their 'false selves' does it become possible for them to attend to the unmet emotional needs gnawing at them from within.

For his part, Wayne Muller observes:

> the persistent questions that occupy the heart of the wounded child are invariably the same questions pondered by the saints, seekers, and spiritual teachers of the world: Why must we have pain? Where do we belong? What is most important in our lives? How can we recognize what is beautiful and true? How may we be joyful? How do we learn to love?[3]

'For wounded children,' Muller tells us, 'these questions are deeply felt but hard to ask and impossible to answer.' Living largely inside themselves and often alone, these children become very aware of 'the nuances of behavior that circle within and around relationships – unable to master them.'[4]

And so, in seeking answers to such ineffable questions, depression plays hide and seek with grandiosity as wounded children search for the unconditional love they never received as children – bouncing back and forth from manic activity to self-doubt, looking for love in 'all the wrong places'.

Of course, such strategies never work very well because, as Alice Miller and Wayne Muller take pains to explain, there is no bypassing the grief of lost innocence. Eventually we all must accept the fact that our losses in childhood cannot be undone. And that it is only through grieving that they can be reframed in the light of maturity, and, thereby, relieved of their exaggerated effects on our lives.

Miller puts it succinctly when she says, 'The greatest of wounds – not to have been loved just as one truly was – cannot heal without the work of mourning.'[5]

Fiona Gardner, in *The Only Mind Worth Having*, qualifies this tragic view of childhood trauma in the light of more recent non-pathologizing approaches to psychotherapy:

> No matter what has happened either in childhood or as an adult, there remains hidden within each person the spirit of

the child. There remains the potential 'to become.' In the relationship with God this spirit of the child is needed, for it brings inherent creativity, spontaneity, and the capacity to live in the moment without self-consciousness.[6]
(see Luke 18.17)

She continues:

Christ is an exemplar for what is being called in this book the *child mind* where the spirit of the child meets the adult experience to produce a new perception. We are asked to become like Christ, we are invited to step out of our prison and to become free. Part of leaving captivity is to release the hidden or secret life of the wounded child – there is an invitation to be born again. If the past can be repaired, at least in part, then there is freedom to live in the present.[7]
(see Matthew 18.1–6; Mark 10.13–16)

The summer before entering Cambridge (1933), Merton revisited Rome. He had been to Rome before, shortly after his father had died in 1931. During that first visit he had hurried around the city, visiting the Forum and other ancient sites. But this time he discovered the early Christian Rome and spent his time visiting churches, admiring Christian icons, crosses, shrines and mosaics.

In fact, it was while gazing at a mosaic of Jesus that Merton first saw Christ through a different set of eyes. Up to that moment he had been more or less an agnostic, yet shortly after contemplating the mosaic, he experienced the 'presence' of his dead father as if he were alive, right there in his rented room, and 'felt pierced deeply with a light' (*SSM*, p. 123). 'And now for the first time in my life,' Merton tells us,

I really began to pray. Praying not with my lips and with my intellect and my imagination but praying out of the very roots of my life and my being and praying to the God I had never known, to reach down towards me out of the darkness and to

help me get free of the thousand terrible things that held my will in their slavery.
(*SSM*, p. 123)

And yet despite this epiphany, his socio-economic privileges and his intellectual precociousness, Merton entered Clare College, Cambridge, a troubled, rootless young man, forced to leave after his first year: besides flunking most of his classes and losing his scholarship, he participated in a mock crucifixion at a drunken fraternity party where he played the role of the crucified.

He also impregnated one of the dormitory staff. A paternity suit was avoided through a monetary settlement, and Merton returned to Douglaston, New York, at the insistence of his godfather – Thomas Bennet – Merton's uncle, namesake and executor of his father's estate.

It may seem odd that Merton's traumatic childhood and troubled adolescence were not more fully treated in his autobiography *The Seven Storey Mountain* (1948). But emotional trauma takes its toll in many ways, including scattered and partial memories, so it wasn't until a few years later that Merton was able to write about 'The Party' in an unpublished novel (*The Labyrinth*). And years before he wrote about fathering a child (which was deleted from *The Seven Storey Mountain* by church censors).[8]

Merton met with psychotherapists a couple of times as an adult, but the most important healing from these traumas of childhood and adolescence came from his undergraduate liberal arts education at Columbia. There Merton found himself 're-parented' by a cohort of brilliant professors and remarkable friends. This was followed by eight years of spiritual direction at Gethsemani where he prayed, wrote in a journal and sweated out most of what remained of his deeply burdened false self. (See *The Sign of Jonas* for an almost day-by-day account of those years of recovery and spiritual rehabilitation.)

Questions for discussion and reflection

1 Looking back over your life, have any of the difficulties, mistakes or losses changed you for the better?

2 What is the story that your family and/or community tells about itself? About you? Are they true?

3 Were you a 'rebel' in secondary school or a 'nerd', 'athlete' or a 'trouble-maker'? (Feel free to supply your own descriptor if none of these apply.) How did these labels affect you? (If this question triggers you emotionally, skip it or take a few minutes to calm and support your inner teenager before proceeding.)

4 Does it help to know that even the celebrated 'spiritual master' Thomas Merton has made big mistakes in his life? How so?

5 What role has memory played in your life? Has it been mostly a burden or a benefit? A little of both?

6

Columbia

The young know they are wretched, for they are full of the truthless ideals which have been instilled in them, and each time they come in contact with the real they are bruised and wounded . . . They must discover for themselves that all they have read and all they have been told are lies, lies, lies; and each discovery is another nail driven into the body on the cross of life.
(Somerset Maugham, *Of Human Bondage*)

We must provide an education that strengthens us against the noise, the violence, and the half-truths of our materialistic society.
(Thomas Merton, *DQ*)

After Merton left Cambridge, he returned to New York, and after taking a term off, travelling and living with his maternal grandparents in Douglaston, Long Island, he enrolled at Columbia College the following January (1935). There he attempted to pick up where he had left off, throwing himself into a blur of activities – joining the Communist Party, pledging to the fraternity Alpha Delta Phi, trying out for the cross-country team, and writing for both the *Columbia Review* and the satirical magazine *The Jester* (where he contributed stories, poems and racy cartoon sketches of female students), all the while listening to the hippest jazz records he could get his hands on, sporting a tweed jacket and smoking a pipe.

As unpromising as all this may sound, it was at Columbia that Merton met Professor Mark Van Doren who eventually became his mentor and turned Merton's attention away from the party scene to the Great Books.

Columbia was also where Merton met a group of talented friends that included the abstract expressionist painter Ad Reinhart, poet Robert Lax, future editor James Laughlin, hipster Seymour Freedgood, and future Merton biographer Ed Rice. They would remain close friends for the rest of his life.

But it took a few years of 'acting out' before Merton could admit that he had become – as he put it in *The Seven Storey Mountain* – 'an extremely unpleasant sort of a person – vain, self-centered, dissolute, weak, irresolute, undisciplined, sensual, obscene and proud . . . a man with veins full of poison, living in death' (*SSM*, p. 132).

It was a harsh appraisal – perhaps too harsh – but it opened him up to the intellectual 're-birth' Columbia College was offering. And Merton was smart and self-aware enough to seize the opportunity. His later conversion to Catholicism at the age of 23 (November 1938) further deepened Merton's 'unlearning' of the tedious and pretentious false self he had wilfully created for himself. And it was by 'unknowing' this hipster that he uncovered 'a prodigal son' within himself who was seeking his way back to the father.

It was Merton's English professor, the writer and critic Mark Van Doren, who had the single most healing influence on Merton. Not only did he deepen Merton's interest in literature, religion and history, he became a role model turning Merton's attention away from the frenzied idleness of the pop culture of the 1930s towards the perennial and 'substantial' questions raised by Shakespeare, Aldous Huxley, Jacques Martian and Étienne Gilson.

Van Doren was a dedicated college teacher who saw liberal education as a way of giving the young a second chance at life through a secular conversion from materialistic careerist concerns to an interest in 'the best that has been thought and said in the world' (*LL*, p. 3). Merton later wrote:

> The thing I liked best about Columbia was the sense that the university was on the whole glad to turn me loose in its library, its classrooms, among its distinguished faculty, and let me make what I liked out of it all. I did. And I ended up being turned on like a pinball machine by Blake, Thomas Aquinas,

Augustine, Eckhart, Coomaraswamy, Traherne, Hopkins, and sacraments of the Catholic Church.
(*LL*, p. 13)

Moreover,

Instead of preparing me for one of those splendid jobs (on Madison Avenue), Columbia cured me forever of wanting one. Instead of adapting me to the world downtown, Columbia did me the favor of lobbing me half-conscious into the Village, where I occasionally came to my senses and where I continued to learn.
(*LL*, pp. 11–12)

In short, Columbia strengthened him 'against the noise, the violence, and the half-truths of our materialist society' (*DQ*, p. 148).

Merton attributed Van Doren's success as a teacher to the fact that he was 'absolutely sincere with generation after generation of students' (*SSM*, p. 153) and that 'his clear mind looked directly for the quiddities of things and sought being and substance under the covering of accident and appearance'. Literature for Van Doren was something more than literature – a chance to see through another person's eyes and vicariously live other lives, and, thereby, discover for oneself who one was and what one really believed (*SSM*, p. 155).

How did Van Doren accomplish this small miracle? Merton tells us:

Most of the time, he asked questions, and his questions were very good, and if you tried to answer them intelligently, you found yourself saying excellent things that you did not know you knew, and that you had not, in fact, known before ... [He] made your mind produce its own ideas.
(*SSM*, p. 154)

Van Doren's Thomist version of the Socratic method would also become Merton's own strategy as a writer and disciple of the *via negativa*.

James Joyce, one of Merton's favourite writers at the time, taught that our interior lives and moral character evolve through a series of what he called *epiphanies*: life-altering moments of comprehension and inner recognition, when we suddenly see ourselves in a new light due to an unexpected event, realization or loss. And in this sudden shift in self-conception, there emerges a sadder but wiser soul.

For Joyce, these epiphanies mark the stages of our psychological maturation – as in the short story *Araby* when a 12-year-old boy's 'crush' on his best friend's 14-year-old sister is not reciprocated no matter what he does. After a humiliation attempting to impress the girl by buying her a gift, he realizes that he is reaching for something that cannot be, and so he accepts the fact that he is still just a child and will remain one for a while longer. In accepting this loss, he finds himself growing up a little bit, and as readers we are reminded of similar turning points in our own lives.

For Joyce, it was the writer's task to narrate such 'epiphanies' with accuracy and compassion – like God – 'present everywhere but visible nowhere'. And if done with accuracy and honesty, such literature could lead to the creation of 'the uncreated conscience of the race'.

But as much as Merton admired Joyce and his doctrine of the epiphany, his own personal experiences of inner transformation had taught him quite a different story. They had led him to believe that we do not have to create a conscience for ourselves because 'we are already born with one. And no matter how much we may ignore it, we cannot silence its insistent demand that we do good and avoid evil' (*NM*, pp. 41–2).

This is the critical difference between the modernist Joyce and the non-modernist Merton: for Merton, 'coming of age' meant following the promptings that came from his own 'true self'; whereas, for Joyce, 'coming of age' was an initiation into the project of existential self-creation.

In this sense, Merton the convert sought the reverse of Stephen Daedalus. Stephen dreamed of going one better than Aquinas, Merton of returning to him. Stephen sought to forge in the smithy of his soul the uncreated conscience of his race. Merton understood that he didn't have to create a conscience for himself because he was born with one. His soul did not have to be forged by experience; it came already intact. But he hadn't quite known that yet because his mind had been colonized by the mock-heroic scepticism of the rationalistic and materialistic age into which he was born.

Questions for reflection and discussion

1 What is the best piece of wisdom anyone has ever shared with you?
2 Who is someone that you have looked up to as a teacher or role model? What did you learn from them? Has your view of their influence changed over the years?
3 Was young adulthood a particularly important phase in your self-development? For better or for worse? A little of both? Explain.

7
Conversion

The Christian does not learn a new set of unworldly laws which he opposes to the way of the world, but by the Cross, the love of Christ, and the indwelling spirit of freedom, he learns to live in the world as Christ did, in perfect liberty and with unlimited compassion and service.
(Thomas Merton , 'Seven Words: The World', in *LL*)

Merton's life at Columbia and later graduate school at Saint Bonaventure were some of the most fruitful years of his life. He began publishing reviews in reputable newspapers and wrote several novels – one of which was published posthumously in 1969 – not to mention publishing a poetry collection for New Directions.

But the exact details of his conversion to Catholicism remain scattered. As it reads in *The Seven Storey Mountain*, it was primarily the product of reading a few books and taking some classes, and then the Church found him. But there must have been more going on than that.

Granted Merton does mention deeply transforming experiences in prayer, including the visitation from his dead father while he was touring Rome in 1933, not to mention reading Gilson's *The Spirit of Medieval Philosophy*. But these epiphanies only seem to confirm my sense that Merton didn't really know how it happened himself. His life-changing transformation from a cynical, self-centred intellectual to a God-fearing contemplative in the short span of two or three years still seems nothing less than a small miracle.

Not that it wasn't primed by his difficult childhood and troubled adolescence, but you would think a writer with his skills would be able to paint a more specific and intimate story of his conversion –

maybe not a road to Damascus experience, but at least a more cogent psychological narrative.

Like many converts, Merton came to the Church on his knees. Merton, it seems, just got fed up with himself, with his presumptions and, perhaps, even with certain aspects of his intellectual rebirth at Columbia. Van Doren's deeply held humanism clearly inspired Merton, but it may have struck him as needing a deeper, more fundamental grounding than neo-Kantian scholasticism – something a little more theologically challenging, like the full-blown mysticism of St John of the Cross, something that could be lived and not just written or spoken about – something that would force him to live beyond his clever means and blow his mind so he could live as an intellectually free man – absolutely paradoxically, teleologically placed.

But nowhere could I find any such confession – not in the journals or the letters. The closest I could find to an explicit rendering of such a turning point in Merton's life trajectory was Merton's letter to Mark Van Doren – but that letter is dated 30 March 1948, the same year *The Seven Storey Mountain* was published and a good ten years *after* Merton was received into the Roman Catholic Church.

The Seven Storey Mountain is a particular puzzle in this regard since the entire book is the narrative of his conversion to Roman Catholicism and the contemplative life, and yet there is no specific passage describing where or when his final inward conversion took place – not even much speculation as to what drove him to go to Mass, talk to priests or read religious books. It all appears to be a puzzle to him, a series of gestures that take him step by step out of the empty, mass-media culture that socialized him, all of which add up to one larger move.

We know that the church censors excised Merton's account of his Cambridge years. And the novel in which he describes 'the party' where he played the role of Christ in a drunken re-enactment of the crucifixion was never published (although drafts are available in the Merton archive). The traumatic years of his childhood are similarly shrouded in the scattered shadows of vague memories of people and events he seemed unready to think about at the time – his bohemian father, his 'distant' mother – and all the blame he levels upon himself. He was, he tells us, 'Nobody's dream child' (*SSM*, p. 5).

So whatever happened to Merton didn't happen when he was writing, and I suspect it didn't happen when he was reading either. There seems to be no single life-changing moment for him, like the epiphany of Stephen Daedalus walking through the cabbage field behind his parents' house. Merton describes his conversion experience more as a crumbling away of his false 'faith' in modernism, with its rational egoism and philosophical scepticism, which had been dimming his imagination and troubling his faith.

Merton's friend and fellow monk John Eudes Bamberger describes Merton's conversion:

> I think it was a gradual thing, but I think too he had an encounter with God and he sensed that God knew him at his worst and his best, and that God loved him. I think Merton's deepest sense of who he was, was that he was a sinner whom God had found and forgiven and made a son. I don't think he was so bad in his youth, but he sensed it as so bad after he had a series of experiences, beginning in Rome, of a very pure vision of God and man. He came to recognize it as a very elevated and high call and that he had been unfaithful to God. He knew too that he should have responded better in his youth but didn't. And therefore, judged himself by a very high standard.[1]

As a result, Merton's writing only got more personal and reflective over his lifetime, describing where his soul had been as well as where it was going. From this period onwards, his works only got more speculative, intuitive and credible. For this was a Merton freed from all his youthful self-suspicions – his doubts about orthodoxy, his personal worthiness, even the authenticity of his faith. This Merton knew what he was talking about because he was talking about his God-given share of the Absolute – beholding his own true

self hidden with Christ in God. Theology by self-discovery and dis-
closure was to be the new wine he poured into new wineskins.

His last abbot, Flavian Burns, confirms this intuition:

> Some ask if Merton was a man who wrestled with God; was
> it a struggle for him or a great love affair? Well, I believe that
> it was simply the consciousness of God and God's purpose
> in the world that permeated Merton's personality and his
> writings, and I think that is why he was autobiographical in
> his nature. He realized himself to be a divine mystery; God
> created him; God had called him into being. He had a divine
> meaning, and he was existential enough to grapple with this
> in his own person and his own life. I think that's why he's so
> attractive to most people, because people feel an affinity with
> that. They realize that he's not just talking for himself. I've had
> many, many people tell me that they read such and such in
> Merton, and they say, 'That's not Merton, that's me; that's my
> own life.'[2]

Questions for reflection and discussion

1 Do you consider yourself a religious 'convert?' If so, was it a
   gradual transition or a more sudden change? Explain.
2 What do you think James Finley meant by calling Thomas
   Merton an 'icon of brokenness'? Is Christ an icon of brokenness?
   Are you?
3 What are the gifts you have not yet brought forward into your
   life? What is holding you back?

8

My Argument with the Gestapo

It is true that Storytelling reveals meaning without committing the error of defining it, that it brings about content and reconciliation with things as they really are, and that we may even trust it to contain eventually by implication that last word which we expect from the 'day of judgment'.
(Hannah Arendt, *Men in Dark Times*)

The first full literary expression of the effect of Merton's conversion can best be seen in his novel, *My Argument with the Gestapo*. Although written in 1941 just six months before Merton entered the monastery at Gethsemani, it wasn't published until 28 years later, at the height of the Vietnam War (1969).

John Leonard, the widely respected book critic for the *New York Times*, described it thus:

More than a surprise, this book is an astonishment. Equal parts autobiography, spiritual passage and incantatory tour de force, less a conventional novel than the word-drunk, panic-stricken, sorrowful-hilarious journal of a man hounded by and hounding after the idea of God.[1]

Mary Gordon, the Catholic novelist, essayist and teacher, devoted an entire chapter of her book *On Thomas Merton* to *My Argument with the Gestapo*, pointing out that it contained in a 'concentrated form the subjects that would dominate Merton's writing and his life: the problem of war and violence, his particular calling as a writer, and his vexed identity as an American whose imagination had been formed in and marked by Europe'.[2]

There is, she adds, 'woven through the text like a pastel thread', the subject of 'Merton, the convert, making his way through the world with a new anointing'.

The story's protagonist and narrator – a character named 'Thomas Merton' – travels from the USA to London and Paris, not as a journalist but as a *novelist*, looking for clues 'as to his own role and responsibilities' in a world torn apart by authoritarian despots, extremist political parties and fascist intimidation.

But the novel is not about Nazi violence per se, but rather something very different. It is, Merton tells us, about 'the Germany that accepted the Nazis' and 'the universal human crisis' of which the Nazis themselves are but 'a partial symptom'.

In the author's Preface, written in 1968, Merton describes it as

a kind of sardonic meditation on the world in which I then found myself: an attempt to define its predicament and my own place in it . . . I did not claim to have gained full access to the whole myth of Europe and the West, only to my own myth.

This 'personal' myth initially inscribed in *My Argument with the Gestapo* is the story of a man of faith thrown haphazardly into the treacheries of a violent, war-torn century that eventually matured into the conversion story of *The Seven Storey Mountain* (1948), his non-fiction sequel to this novel of origins, which was followed by his series of devotional classics in the 1950s and his prophetic essays, letters and journals in the 1960s.

And yet, the wry observations of Merton the young convert still strike a chord with us today because they anticipated the struggles of several generations of Americans – ourselves included – against the authoritarian and totalitarian forces of the modern age. Like the young Merton, we have had to perpetually reconsider our roles and responsibilities as free men and women living amid an onslaught of propaganda and mass-mediated sentimentality unleashed upon us from all directions and by all manner of con-artists, ideologues, public relations 'experts' and true believers.

We now know – much better than Merton did in 1941 – exactly how far fascist distortions can go. But we seem to have forgotten – or perhaps never learned – exactly how to defend ourselves against the demagogues that fuel such jingoism in the first place.

If we are not to lose our *own* argument with the Gestapo, we would do well to begin where Merton himself began – bearing witness to what it means to live a life in the truth by speaking plainly without recourse to platitudes, ideological jargon or special pleading.

In one scene, 'Merton' is being interrogated by a military patrol as to why he is in London and what he's writing. The officer seems sceptical when 'Merton' tells him he is writing *a novel* and not advocacy journalism. 'Merton' replies, 'The opinions of politicians and soldiers have no meaning for me. But there must be other meanings, on another level, and I have come back to look for them' (*MA*, p. 28).

When the soldiers ask him who he is, he replies,

I am a writer. I write what I see out the window. I am writing about the fear on the faces of the houses . . . And I write that the houses of bombarded London do not understand their own fear.
(*MA*, p. 52)

The soldiers then ask him why he confuses fear with courage, and Merton replies: 'I am still trying to find out: and that is why I write.' When one of the soldiers asks how writing can possibly help him to find out, Merton offers a succinct description of his early sense of vocation:

I will keep putting things down until they become clear. (And if they do not become clear?) I will have a hundred books full of symbols, full of everything I ever knew or ever saw or ever thought . . . Some things are too clear to be understood, and what you think is your understanding of them is only a kind of charm, a kind of incantation in your mind concerning that

thing. This is not understanding: it is something you remember. So much for definition! We always have to go back and start from the beginning and make over all the definitions for ourselves again.
(*MA*, pp. 52–3)

A patrolwoman hands him a note with her phone number on it and tells him, 'Come and see me when I am not so tired. Maybe I will remember how to talk' (*MA*, p. 28). This is not, as it may at first seem, a flirtatious come-on so much as an admission that, given her current role as a security officer, it is impossible for her to speak with 'Merton' with any candour as a *human being*, and yet her encounter with him has reminded her of that latent possibility.

In another scene, 'Merton' confesses to his own difficulties writing:

I wish everything I wrote would be able to be read most of all by children and nuns and holy people, but then I know I am crazy to expect that, because I have trailed around in the dirt too much to please them, they are happy and good and talk straighter than I because they haven't got so much pride to try to work into humility one way or another.
(*MA*, p. 189)

If the book seemed oddly out of place in 1941, perhaps that was because its time (our time) had not yet come.

Questions for reflection and discussion

1 It's been said that life makes sense looking backwards but must be lived going forwards. Do you think this is true? Does the telling of it in retrospect obscure the radical changes you experienced while living it?
2 What kind of story is the newly converted Merton telling here? How would you characterize it?
3 Do you identify with the narrator? Why or why not?

9

Escape from escapism

We are called to share with God the work of creating the truth
of our identity.
(Thomas Merton, *NS*)

Merton decided to enter a monastery rather than work full time in
Dorothy Van Hueck's Harlem settlement house because he thought
the monk's vows of poverty, chastity and obedience better fulfilled
his desire to 'give God everything' (*SSM*, pp. 399–401).

But when the Franciscans delayed (and ultimately denied)
his application, it would take almost another year before he was
accepted by the Trappists at Gethsemani Monastery in Bardstown,
Kentucky.

Merton described his gratitude for being accepted in this famous
prayer from the closing pages of *The Seven Storey Mountain*:

> You have brought me here [the Abbey of Gethsemani] not to
> wear a label by which I can recognize myself and place myself
> in some kind of category. You do not want me thinking about
> what I am, but about what You are. Or rather, You do not even
> want me to be thinking about anything much: for You would
> raise me above the level of thoughts. And if I am always trying
> to figure out what I am and where I am and why I am, how will
> that work get done?

He then hears God's reply:

> I will give you what you desire. I will lead you into solitude. I
> will lead you by the way that you cannot possibly understand
> because I want it to be the quickest way. Therefore, all the

things around you will be armed against you, to deny you, to hurt you, to give you pain, and therefore to reduce you to solitude.
(*SSM*, p. 461)

Merton is reporting here on how God did, in fact, respond to his prayer. For, despite the picaresque view of monasticism promoted by his publisher at the time, becoming a monk was quite difficult for Merton. Not just because of the rigorous physical demands of the Trappist way of life, but also because of the numerous physical and medical ailments he had to endure. By the age of 35, Merton had lost most of his teeth and hair and suffered everything from bursitis to colitis and arthritis, skin problems and a bad back.

He also struggled with the fact that his abbot, Father Dom James Fox, did not share many of his views, restricted his travel, and later, after his vows, even accused him of narcissism, suggesting he see a psychotherapist. Dom James was an all-American Catholic who loved football and came from the University of Notre Dame, while Merton, as we have seen, was European born and a child of bohemian artists, who wrote poetry and avant-garde novels in his spare time and read books of cutting-edge literature and theology in the languages of their origin.

It took many years but their relationship did improve. Dom James eventually appointed Merton to the position of novice master and later helped him to live as a hermit on monastery grounds. He was also quite compassionate in his dealing with Merton's clandestine relationship with a student nurse he had met while recuperating from back surgery. (By all accounts a relatively chaste high school 'crush' for the middle-aged Father Louie.)

For his part, Merton complained about travel restrictions but took them gracefully as a dutiful monk under obedience, describing monastic life as a 'school of charity'. Merton had intended to give up writing upon entering the monastery, but this was never really an option given the many writing tasks he was assigned. And Merton found himself composing poems as part of his morning meditations.

Abbot Flavian Burns – Dom James's successor – speculates that the reason Dom James hadn't allowed Merton to travel was not out of jealousy of Merton's fame but because he did not want people to meet the outgoing, casual Merton, the Merton who did not take himself seriously, because it might undermine the image readers had of him as a brooding and isolated mystic. Meeting the 'real' Thomas Merton might just undermine the Trappist 'brand'.[1]

Matthew Kelty, one of Merton's fellow monks at Gethsemani, described his first impression of Merton as a precocious young man who had suffered a miserable 'wandering' childhood, never having a real home:

> He had a lot of sadness, and you'd see it in his face if you knew when to look. Some of his pictures reveal it . . . There's a certain sadness in him at the beginning of his monastic life. But all monks have known suffering. That is where they get their wisdom from.[2]

As we have already seen, Merton wrote his early novels in a Joycean key – a reverse Stephen Daedalus in a way. But his poetry grew out of his reading of William Blake and Gerald Manley Hopkins. Just as his essays grew out of his wrestling with the ideas of Aldous Huxley, St Augustine and Étienne Gilson. It was while travelling alone in Italy that Merton first saw Christ through new, awakened eyes as he was depicted in an ancient mosaic. But it was in Cuba that he met the Holy Mother, who made her presence known to him at the St Francis Church in Havana, and it was in this moment that his mind moved into his heart in a settled love and consolation.

In the 1950s, Merton became master of scholastics at Gethsemani and published a series of devotional books on contemplative themes – most notably *No Man is an Island* (1955), *Thoughts in Solitude* (1958) and *New Seeds of Contemplation* (1961). In these books Merton revealed his contemplative view of Catholicism as best understood – not as a rigid theological system that contained answers to every question, but as an initiation into the questions one needs to ask if one is to transform one's life from one of conformity, passivity and consumption to one of discovery, surprise and spiritual clairvoyance.

'Christianity is more than a doctrine,' Merton wrote.

> It is Christ Himself, living in those whom He has united to Himself in one Mystical Body. It is the mystery by which the Incarnation of the Word of God continues and extends itself throughout the history of the world, reaching into the souls and lives of all men, until the final completion of God's plan. Christianity is the 're-establishment of all things in Christ' (Ephesians 1:10).
>
> (*LB*, p. ix)

By the early 1960s he was corresponding with a host of international writers and thinkers of many faiths and diverse traditions – from the Hasidim to Sufis to Frankfurt School critical theorists. His correspondence with D. T. Suzuki blossomed into a lifelong interest in Zen Buddhism which took him to Asia in 1968 to attend an international conference of both Christian and Buddhist contemplatives.

It was on this trip that Merton met the Dalai Lama, Chogyam Trungpa and other Tibetan Buddhist exiles. And it was on this trip that he died by accidental electrocution in Thailand.

The suddenness of his departure punctuated the radical contingency of his life, emphasizing its existential unpredictability. His unredacted journals and letters would eventually be published and absorb the world's attention after the fact. All this would have probably seemed to Merton – had he the power to comment from the beyond – as a distraction from the momentum of his life's ever forward-charging trajectory towards the numinous.

Two months before, when Merton had set out on this final journey, the poet Ron Seitz drove Merton to the airport. Seitz remembers his last conversation with Merton:

> He looked at me directly, but in a very relaxed gentle way (unlike his usual intense, almost open stare), and softly,

slowly . . . (as best as I can 'catch it' in memory) . . . 'You know, if God is really here, in this room, in this place – as we know he is, eh . . .we can't be in too much trouble, now can we?

'See. Either we are one with the Holy Spirit, or not. Eh? And if the incarnation, the "Word Made Flesh", is a living reality – then the whole cosmos is sacramentalized . . . is sacred and holy . . . is redeemed – is really Church. See [smiling] . . . and you can't get out, eh, can't escape that . . . even if you wanted to.

'So, you see, you don't really need to get anywhere or be anybody – all that so-called ambition and "going somewhere" thing . . . you're already who you are and where you are: home! . . . really – God's house, eh? . . . Creation.

'Now – as we've said so many times before – you've got to stop all this stuff about just-i-fi-ca-tion . . . Let go and be who you have always been! That's the one-time, most important thing you've got to remember to remember. That's the true meaning of *resurrection* . . . a return to your original source – God home to God.

'So – again I want to remind you – stop trying to be other than who you are by erecting monuments of your achieve-ments – such things as books, artworks, great ideas . . . you know: evidence to prove your worth and justify your existence to God. That's all so much waste.

'See. That's the true meaning of *hope* . . . to trust in the ultimate goodness of creation. Hope doesn't mean an antici-pation or expectation of deliverance from an intolerable or oppressive situation or condition . . . That's what most of us are doing most of the time: wanting something other than what is. As I said – true hope is trusting that what we have, where we are, and who we are is more than enough for us creatures of God.

'To appreciate this, you've got to know that *revelation* is all around you all the time. Revelation expressing itself as beauty, truth, goodness, and especially love!'[3]

Questions for reflection and discussion

1 Sometimes people's lives look different to us after they die. This can be seen in the lives of public figures such as Mother Teresa, Dorothy Day, Pope John Paul II, even Michael Jackson. Think of a few famous people who have died during your lifetime. Or friends and family who have passed away. Did their lives look different to you after they were gone? In what way?

2 How did you decide what you wanted to do with your life? Have you decided on a calling or career, or are you standing at a cross-roads? Explain.

3 Rather than ask yourself what you want to do, try asking yourself what you are willing to suffer for? Is there a difference? Explain.

10

The Seven Storey Mountain

The truth is I am far from being the monk or cleric that I ought
to be. My life is a great mess and tangle of half-conscious sub-
terfuges to evade grace and duty.
(Thomas Merton, *SJ*)

As noted earlier, one of the writing assignments Merton was given
by his advisors at Gethsemani – an autobiographical essay – blossomed into the book-length memoir that became the international
bestseller *The Seven Storey Mountain* (1948). Within a year of its
publication, the 33-year-old Thomas Merton had become the most
famous monk in American history.

He was uncomfortable with the celebrity and spent the next 20
years trying to live it down. Shortly after the book's publication,
Merton declared its author 'dead', and denounced the book's strict
Manichean division between sacred and secular experience and its
facile dismissal of other faiths as the kind of religious extremism
common to the newly converted.

Nevertheless, *The Seven Storey Mountain* continued (and continues) to inspire new converts to Christianity and new postulants to
the monastic life – in part because of its perennial themes and in
part because it was written in a different key from the flood of other
post-war cultural reappraisals. It was a compelling first-person
description of the clash between his transcendent aspirations as an
individual and the demands of contemporary economic, political
and technological systems. Moreover, Merton's critique had a surprising and unexpected conclusion in which his soul triumphed
over its circumstances through a return to contemplative living.

People expect a monk to talk about religion, but Merton knew
revealed religion could only be communicated poetically, so he

described his frightening French boarding school, his travels to cathedrals in Rome and Cuba, his troubled years at Cambridge, and what it felt like reading James Joyce and William Blake, attending Columbia College, going to nightclubs in Harlem, and how the dawn broke over the Kentucky hills. And through all this, his readers discovered what it meant to be a believer, a Catholic and a contemplative. It meant being everything, for everything belonged to the grace of God.

The year *The Seven Storey Mountain* was published, George Orwell began writing *1984*, Norman Mailer published *The Naked and the Dead*, and a cadre of thinkers that included Eric Fromm, Aldous Huxley, D. T. Suzuki, Czeslaw Milosz, Boris Pasternak, Henry Miller, Jacques Maritain, James Baldwin, Walker Percy, Louis Zukofsky, Dorothy Day and Dan Berrigan were all considering the fate of the individual amid new forms of totalitarianism, propaganda and psycho-social control.

Unlike so many of these critiques of nascent authoritarianism, *The Seven Storey Mountain* not only offered a defence of individual conscience but it also provided an unexpected return to contemplative religious sources, bringing the wisdom of monasticism to bear upon contemporary life with fresh insight.

The book was hailed by post-war converts, cradle Catholics, sceptics and agnostics alike – indeed by the entire panoply of post-war religious seekers, including Jews, Catholics and Protestants, as well as Buddhists, Baptists and beatniks.

Merton was celebrated as a modern Augustine who understood – in a way no one had yet been able to so convincingly express – that modernity may have lifted us above the level of the world's concerns but not delivered us from them. And so stronger medicine was needed, the medicine of a counter-cultural, contemplative way of life.

In a letter to Mark Van Doren (30 March 1948), written the same year *The Seven Storey Mountain* was published, Merton described his evolving sense of vocation:

I can no longer see the ultimate meaning of a man's life in terms of either 'being a poet' or 'being a contemplative' or even in a

54

certain sense 'being a saint' (although that is the only thing to be). It must be something much more immediate than that. I – and every other person in the world – must say: 'I have my own special, peculiar destiny which no one else ever has had or ever will have. There exists for me a peculiar goal, a fulfilment which must be all my own – nobody else's – & it does not really identify that destiny to put it under some category – "poet," "monk," "hermit." Because my own individual destiny is a meeting, an encounter with God that He has destined for me alone. His glory in me will be to receive from me something He can never receive from anyone else –because it is a gift of His to me which He has never given to anyone else & never will. My whole life is only that – to establish that particular constant with God which is the one He has planned for my eternity!' (*RJ*, p. 22)

Merton followed up *The Seven Storey Mountain* (1948) with *Seeds of Contemplation* (1948), a guide to contemplative prayer, but didn't write another autobiographical work (unless you count some of his poems) until seven years later when he published selections from his journal entries in *The Sign of Jonas* (1953), a book that charted the early years of Merton's monastic life.

The monastic scholar Jean LeClerq criticized *The Sign of Jonas* without even reading it. In a letter to Merton he expressed his view that monks should not write books about themselves for any reason. Merton replied by asking LeClerq if he hadn't wished Bernard of Clairvaux had left a record of his own personal reflections and experiences? LeClerq wasn't convinced.

It was only after LeClerq heard passages from *The Sign of Jonas* being read aloud in an African monastery that he had to admit to himself that Merton's writing was certainly valuable and changed his mind about monks writing books about themselves.[1]

By now it should have been clear that Thomas Merton had converted to a church of monks and reformers decidedly more counter-cultural than the dogmatic pieties of establishment priests and culturally imperialistic missionaries.

Merton found himself bringing contemplative Christianity into dialogue with what Dietrich Bonhoeffer had called a 'world come of age', a world increasingly beholden to the technological fix, a world in which religious discourse had less and less of a bearing on practical life.

Merton's conversion told a different story: that it was still possible to follow one's conscience, outgrow one's false self, find God in the process, and live in humble gratitude for the ignorant perfection of one's own true self – in opposition to the deformations of character and community generated by the false idols of contemporary militarism, materialism and monomania.

The Seven Storey Mountain had somehow broken through the cynicism and ennui of its times by inspiring readers to think 'outside' economic and political co-ordinates as the primary contexts of their lives to consider the possibility that they might not have been created to fit into this world, and that they themselves could live an authentically transcendent life of faith without having to give themselves over to the magical thinking of fundamentalism or the 'cheap grace' of sentimental kitsch Catholicism.

For Merton, the contemplative life signalled a radical dissent not only from the status quo but also from the 'blind faith' of the 'true believers' whose unwillingness to face the radical contingency of the human condition reduced Christianity to little more than what Richard Rohr has called a transactional 'cosmic insurance policy' based on the proposition that if I 'believe', God will deliver 'the goods', regardless of the kind of life I live.

As Merton famously remarked in the Preface to a later edition of the book:

By my monastic life and vows I am saying no to all the concentration camps, the aerial bombardments, the staged political trials, the judicial murders, the racial injustices, the economic tyrannies, and the whole socioeconomic apparatus which seems geared for nothing but global destruction in spite of all its fair words in favor of peace.
(*HR*, p. 65)

He continues:

> If there is a 'problem' for Christianity today, it is the prob-
> lem of the identification of 'Christendom' with certain forms
> of culture and society, certain political and social structures
> which for fifteen hundred years have dominated Europe and
> the West. The first monks were men and women, who already
> in the fourth century, began to protest against this identifi-
> cation as a falsehood and a servitude. Fifteen hundred years
> of Western Christendom , in spite of certain definite achieve-
> ments, have not been an unequivocal glory to Christendom.
> The time has come for judgment to be passed on this history.
> I can rejoice in this fact, believing that the judgment will be
> a liberation of the Christian faith from the servitude to and
> involvement in the structures of the secular world. And that
> is why I think certain forms of Christian 'optimism' are to
> be taken with reservations, in so far as they lack a genuine
> eschatological consciousness of the Christian vision and
> concentrate upon the naive hope of merely temporal achieve-
> ments – churches on the moon!
> (*HR*, p. 66)

'What we need', Merton tells us,

> is the gift of God which makes us able to find in ourselves not
> just *ourselves* but *Him*: and then our nothingness becomes His
> all. This is not possible without the liberation effected by com-
> punction and humility. It requires not talent, not mere insight,
> but sorrow, pouring itself out in love and trust.
> (*SSM*, p. 341)

Eloquent words, but what was not yet so apparent to either his
admirers or to his critics (or, perhaps, even to himself) was the
radically counter-cultural implications of his otherwise very
orthodox-sounding conversion story, for it implies a change of al-
legiance from the powerful to the powerless, an actual conversion

of one's manners and way of life as well as one's point of view, some kind of change in living in relationship to the socio-economic order.

Questions for reflection and discussion

1 When you pray, do you ask God to direct the currents of your life towards some specific goal? Or are you trying to understand with compassion and curiosity where the deeper currents of God's will are taking *you*? What is the difference between these two kinds of discernment?

2 Looking at your life, what needs to be brought forward? And what left behind?

3 In what ways does the narrator of *The Seven Storey Mountain* describe a world that we ourselves are still living in? In what ways is it a world we have left behind?

11
What is contemplation?

[T]he true contemplative is not the one who prepares his
mind for a particular message that he wants or expects to hear,
but who remains empty because he knows that he can never
expect or anticipate the word that will transform his darkness
into light. He does not demand light instead of darkness. He
waits on the Word of God in silence.
(Thomas Merton, *CMP*)

We have to travel in the void and be perfectly happy about it.
(Thomas Merton, *HGL*)

For Merton, the search for God is also a search for reality.
Contemplation is the experience of God's living presence within us
'as the transcendent source of our own subjectivity' (*NS*, p. 68). He
describes it in this way:

The contemplative life is a dimension of our subjective existence. Discovering the contemplative life is a new self-discovery.
One might say it is the flowering of a deeper identity on an
entirely different plane from a mere psychological discovery, a
paradoxical new identity that is found only in loss of self.
(*CIWA*, p. 340)

In defining the contemplative life as a 'dimension of our subjective
experience' irreducible to psychological categories, Thomas Merton
challenged all the modern notions of the self, history, identity, being
and theology. This led to his lifelong search for a religious idiom
capable of overcoming the confusions brought about by post-
Enlightenment theological terminology.

Merton wanted *to speak the thing itself* – that is to say, he wanted to speak the language of transfiguring love *directly*, to speak what silence 'says'. This led him to poetry and to phenomenological descriptions of Christian virtues and practices.

> What is the dimension of this depth? It is the incorporation of the unknown and of the unconscious into our daily life. Faith brings together the known and the unknown so that they overlap: or rather, so that we are aware of their overlapping. Actually, our whole life is a mystery of which very little comes to our conscious understanding. But when we accept only what we can consciously rationalize, our life is actually reduced to the most pitiful limitations, though we may think otherwise. (We have been brought up with the absurd prejudice that only what we can reduce to a rational and conscious formula is really understood and experienced in our life. When we can say what a thing is, or what we are doing, we think we fully grasp and experience it. In point of fact this verbalization – very often it is nothing more than verbalization – tends to cut us off from genuine experience and to obscure our understanding instead of increasing it.)
> (*NS*, pp. 138–9)

Thomas Merton often warned against carving out a part of our lives and designating it 'spiritual'. The spiritual life encompasses all aspects of existence – it is not a part of it. To splinter one's life into a life of faith and a life of action (or a life of piety and a life of self-seeking) only confuses things. God alone is the one needful thing. God alone can lead us to our *true selves* – and free us from the proud and misguided attempts we make to master and control the world.

> Contemplative prayer is, in a way, simply the preference for the desert, for emptiness, for poverty . . . Only when we are able to 'let go' of everything within us, all desire to see, to know, to taste and to experience the presence of God, do we

truly become able to experience that presence with the over-
whelming conviction and reality that revolutionizes our entire
inner life.
(*CP*, p. 89)

In speaking for monks, I am really speaking for a very strange
kind of person, a marginal person, because the monk in the
modern world is no longer an established person with an
established place in society . . . The marginal man accepts
the basic irrelevance of the human condition, an irrelevance
which is manifested above all by the fact of death. The marginal person, the monk, the displaced person, the prisoner,
all these people live in the presence of death, which calls into
question the meaning of life.
(*AJ*, pp. 305–6)

He struggles with the fact of death in himself, trying to seek
something deeper than death: because there is something
deeper than death, and the office of the monk or marginal
person, the meditative person or the poet is to go beyond
death even in this life, to go beyond the dichotomy of life and
death and to be therefore, a witness to life.
(*AJ*, p. 306)

For Merton, marginal persons are more likely to trust in God and
the spiritual contour of their lives and to trust less in their wealth,
accomplishments or reputation. They have passed through a psychological boundary where they can begin to live without trying;
that is to say, without trying to fit in, or to be seen, or to matter in
some dramatic or historic way.

The 'I' that works in the world and thinks about itself is not the
true 'I' that has been united to God in Christ. 'Contemplation is
precisely the awareness that this "I" is really "not I" and the awakening of the unknown "I" that is beyond observation and reflection
and is incapable of commenting upon itself' (*NS*, p. 7). Merton
elaborates:

When a man constantly looks and looks at himself in the mirror of his own acts, his spiritual double vision splits him into two people. And if he strains his eyes hard enough, he forgets which one is real. In fact, reality is no longer found either in himself or in his shadow. The substance has gone out of itself into the shadow, and he has become two shadows instead of one real person. Then the battle begins. Whereas one shadow was meant to praise the other, now one shadow accuses the other. The activity that was meant to exalt him, reproaches and condemns him. It is never real enough. Never active enough. The less he is able to *be* the more he has to *do*. He becomes his own slave driver – a shadow whipping a shadow to death, because it cannot produce reality, infinitely substantial reality, out of his own nonentity. (*NM*, pp. 118–20)

This description of a postmodern man – endlessly fabricating with his desires but never satisfied with what he has – is the very definition of an imaginary life. 'And so when they die,' Merton says, 'they will find out that they long ago ceased to exist because God, Who is infinite reality and Whose sight is the being of everything that is, will say to them "I know you not"' (*NS*, p. 50).

It is hard for them to imagine dying fulfilled or with any gratitude for their transitory existence because they remain alone in the isolation of their conceptions of themselves and the unreality of their own imagined failures and achievements now so plainly revealed as fictions. And so if one has never identified with anything greater than one's self, death becomes a confrontation with despair, and the ultimate scientific research project becomes the search for everlasting biological life (never mind who or what becomes immortal).

Merton's 'way' to avoid this self-alienation was to join a monastery. By taking vows of chastity, poverty and obedience, he opened the way to contemplative living by dashing his second 'writerly' self against the rock of his monastic vows. 'Give God everything,' he told himself.

As extreme as this may sound, this 'preference for the desert, for emptiness' was Merton's 'way'. It was both the precondition and the final result of his religious conversion.

Like the men and women who fled to the desert seeking an alternative to empire, the desert tradition preceded the emergence of systematic theology and the formalization of doctrines and creeds. Faith was first a way of living before it was a belief system. In some areas, like Alexandria in Egypt, you had to be a long-standing monk before you could be a bishop, which entirely changed the character of bishops.

These early monks and bishops were probably the link from the desert period to what became the 'Eastern Church'. At first, instead of formulating theology, they told stories much like Jesus did, about the essential issues of ego, love, virtue, surrender, peace, divine union and inner freedom. It was later that they also became much more formalized and argumentative, just like the Church in the West.

Thomas Merton describes those who fled to the wilderness as people 'who did not believe in letting themselves be passively guided and ruled by a decadent state', who didn't wish to be ruled or to rule – people who sought their 'true self, in Christ', and in order to do so they had to reject 'the false self, fabricated under social compulsion "by the world". Their way to God was uncharted and freely chosen, not inherited from others who had mapped it out beforehand' (WOD, p. 56). Merton explains:

> I want to know God in an unknowing and to love him in an unloving, in an indistinct union that becomes identification with and oneness with God. Yes, we are distinct. But my experience of our union is an experience of indistinction, of oneness, of union of identity. To know God is to know that I am one with him and that we have the same being. I am not God but God is in me.[1]

In this sense, Merton's view of contemplation boils down to four key ideas:

1 Contemplation is a *behaviour* – the act of attaining access to a hitherto untapped region of subjective experience. It is spiritual

wonder linked with gratitude for life, awareness and for being, constituting 'the highest expression of man's intellectual and spiritual life' (*NS*, p. 1).

2 Contemplation is a *way of knowing* – 'pure and virginal – poor in concepts, poorer still in reasoning but able by its very poverty and purity to follow the Word wherever He may go' (*NS*, p. 5).

3 Contemplation is a *manifestation* of the 'true self' hidden with Christ in God (Colossians 3.3–4).

> At the center of our being [is] a point of nothingness which is untouched by illusion, a point of pure truth, a point or spark which belongs entirely to God, which is never at our disposal, from which God disposes of our lives which is inaccessible to the fantasies of our own mind and the brutalities of our own will . . . I have no program for this seeing. It is only given. But the gate of heaven is everywhere. (*CGB*, p. 142)

And so . . .

4 A contemplative is a particular *kind of Christian disciple* – someone

> who has risked his mind in the desert beyond language and beyond ideas where God is encountered in the nakedness of true of pure trust, that is to say in the surrender of our poverty and incompleteness in order no longer to clench our minds in a cramp upon themselves, as if thinking made us exist. The message of hope the contemplative offers you, then, brothers and sisters, is not that you need to find your way through the jungle of language and problems that today surround God, but whether you understand or not, God loves you, is present in you, lives in you, dwells in you, calls you, saves you, and offers you an understanding and light which are like nothing you ever found in books or heard in sermons. (*HGL*, p. 158)

Questions for reflection and discussion

1 Much of our time is spent avoiding troubles and inconveniences. How would our lives be different if we weren't problem-solving all the time?

2 Do you know any master craftsmen in the creation of fears? Are you one of them?

3 Have you ever given yourself permission just to feel your feelings rather than judge or fix them?

4 What problem are you currently in the middle of solving that might better be turned over to God?

12

Crossing the Rubicon

> My focus is not on dogmas as such, but only on their repercussions in the life of a soul in which they begin to find a concrete realization. I may be pardoned for using my own words to talk about my own soul.
> (Thomas Merton, *SJ*)

As William H. Shannon pointed out in his biography of Merton, *Silent Lamp*, it wasn't until December 1949 that Merton 'crossed his literary Rubicon', declaring in the Preface to the revised edition of *New Seeds of Contemplation* that from now on he would be writing about spiritual things from the point of view of experience rather than in the concise terms of dogmatic theology. After that, Merton never looked back. He was no longer a man with 'answers' so much as a man with hitherto unasked – and better – questions, testing old formulas 'in the crucible of experience'.[1]

As the late 1950s transformed slowly into the 1960s, Merton began writing more on secular issues and ecumenical themes from a monastic point of view, and in the process he found himself interlocutor and peer to such post-war prodigies as Hannah Arendt, Jean-Paul Sartre, Albert Camus, Aldous Huxley – and later to such counter-culture figures as Alan Watts, Lawrence Ferlinghetti, Norman Mailer, Mary Daly and Herbert Marcuse, including fellow Catholics Dorothy Day, Walker Percy, Marshall McLuhan, Ivan Illich, and Phil and Daniel Berrigan.

This was not a particularly surprising turn of events, for Merton had not converted to the Catholic Church of American Nationalism whose bishops blessed battleships – nor to the Eurocentric Catholic Church that saw America in need of remedial evangelization. He had converted to the anti-imperialist Church of the Desert Fathers and Mothers, whose ranks included an irregular collection of first- and second-century hermits and monks and outsiders, beginning with John the Baptist and continuing through a vanguard of fourth-century seekers who fled the Roman Empire to find God – figures like St Anthony, Gregory of Nyssa, Cassian and Origen, whose ideas continued to evolve through the centuries and had a considerable influence on Merton's own writing.

Looked at retrospectively, Thomas Merton's life could be seen as the story of an aspiring modern novelist who – through writing, contemplation and the fulfilment of his monastic vows – grew a personality that in the end allowed him to transcend art. That is to say, in the process of writing about how he had come to see through the false promises of modernity and the illusions of bourgeois civilization, he turned his attention and his energy to the emancipatory project of a new prophetic brand of contemplative Christianity.

Merton saw the Christian life as a process of self-emptying (kenosis), through which we come to realize that ultimately there is nothing *real* in us that is anything more substantial than God's infinite love, which expresses itself in and through our own true self. In other words, we are called to take on the mind of Christ – the mind of the boundless oneness of love. And so, when we seek what is truest in ourselves and in our traditions, we discover we are one with those who seek what is truest in their sacred traditions, for there is a point of convergence in God where we meet.

But to explain such a revelation to a sceptical world, a convincing critique of modernity is needed, one that explains exactly what went wrong with the separation of facts from values, objects from subjects, us from them, and now from then – a critique Merton had begun but hadn't the time to bring to completion.

In 1967, just a year before he died, Merton wrote this in response to a request from Pope Paul VI for a message from contemplatives to the world. It is worth quoting at length:

> Can I tell you that I have found answers to the questions that torment the [people] of our time? I do not know if I have found answers. When I first became a monk, yes, I was more

sure of 'answers'. But as I grow old in the monastic life and advance further into solitude, I become aware that I have only begun to seek the questions.

Can [we] make sense of our existence? Can we honestly give our lives meaning merely by adopting a certain sense of explanations which pretend to tell [us] why the world began and where it will end, why there is evil and what is necessary for a good life. My brothers and sisters, perhaps, I have become in my solitude an explorer for you, a searcher in realms which you are not able to visit – except perhaps in the company of your psychiatrist.

I have been summoned to explore a desert area of [the human heart] in which explanations no longer suffice, and in which one learns that only experience counts. An arid, rocky, dark land of the soul, sometimes illuminated by strange fires which [we] fear and peopled by spectres which [we] studiously avoid except in [our] nightmares. And in this area I have learned that one cannot truly know hope unless [one] has found out how like despair hope is. The language of Christianity has said this for centuries in other less naked terms.
(*HGL*, pp. 156–7)

Merton had tried to formally articulate the psycho-social implications of his contemplative vision twice: the first time in his theological essay *The Ascent to Truth* (1951), and then again ten years later in *The New Man* (1961). Neither work found much of an audience. So, Merton turned back to writing first-person critical essays, poetry and reflections on contemporary issues and perennial religious controversies and themes.

Questions for discussion and reflection

1 Malcolm X once said, 'Sincerity is my only credential.' Can the same be said for Merton? In what sense can the same be said for all of us?
2 As Merton matured as a monk, he found he had more questions than he did answers. Have you ever experienced being less certain of something the more you knew about it? Give an example.
3 What does experience teach that formulas don't?

13

Merton as spiritual director

Coming to the monastery has been for me exactly the right
kind of withdrawal. It has given me perspective. It has taught
me how to live. And now I owe everyone else in the world a
share of that life.
(Thomas Merton, *SJ*)

Merton was named Master of Scholastics at Gethsemani in 1951.
This made him academic advisor and spiritual director for those
preparing for ordination. In *The Sign of Jonas*, his journal from that
year, he described his new position as an opportunity to dive even
deeper into the heart of his monastic calling:

It is as if I were beginning all over again to be a Cistercian,
but this time I am doing it without asking myself the abstract
questions which are the luxury and the torment of one's
monastic adolescence. For now I am a grown-up monk and
have no time for anything but the essentials. The only essential
is not an idea or an ideal: it is God Himself, who cannot be
found by weighing the present against the future or the past
but only sinking into the heart of the present like it is.
(*SOJ*, p. 330)

The primary problem for the novices, as Merton saw it, had chiefly
to do with 'thoughts' – useless interior activity projected into words
and ideas. By submitting to the authority of a spiritual director,
however, they could protect themselves from certain common idol-
atries. The director reassures them that their minds – although they
appeared full – are really quite empty, and yet at the centre of this
nothingness was something infinitely real.

When I taught at Christian Brothers High School in Sacramento, California, one of the Brothers made a splash at commencement when he told the graduating class, 'I am particularly proud of this group of seniors because I know that many of you have taken the journey to the center of your minds and discovered that it doesn't exist.' Then he sat down (to the chagrin of many tuition-paying parents).

The Brother was making the same point to those high school graduates as Merton is making here to his novices. A spiritual director's job is to persuade his novices to stop trying to run their own lives with the meagre resources of their own minds. Only then will they seek consolation from God – which is a very hard lesson to learn if you have never stopped working on yourself in constant preparation for the future (Matthew 6.28).

This is why the young are so attracted to new methods and novel doctrines; they are outlets for self-expression. The novice master must see through such enthusiasms, advocate humility, and persist even when the student's self-will transforms itself into self-justification or a desire to please. The goal here is not to put the student under the director's command but to develop in them an indifference to both censure and praise.

Merton explains, 'No one teaches contemplation except God, Who gives it. The best you can do is write something or say something that will serve as an occasion for someone to realize what God wants of him' (*NS*, p. 271).

This point is deftly summed up by one of Merton's former students, psychotherapist James Finley. 'Merton's message', he tells us, 'is that every Christian, in his own way as willed by God, must by way of simple faith, selfless love, and humble prayer realize that the nothingness he fears is in fact the treasure he longs for.' He must learn to expect nothing out of anything and everything out of nothing.[1]

Those who entered the order with a contempt for worldly values have it only half right. By turning away from the materialism and cheap thrills of popular culture, they bravely sought God in a desert where the emotions could find nothing to sustain them. 'But this too can be an error,' Merton points out.

> For if our emotions really die in the desert, our humanity dies with them. We must return from the desert like Jesus or St. John with our capacity for feeling expanded and deepened, strengthened against the appeals of falsity, warned against temptation, great, noble and pure.
> (*TIS*, p. 16)

The *return from the desert* became one of Merton's great themes. The decision to join the Trappists was not a rejection of the world per se but a turning towards the true source of being. Turning towards God is a returning to the true self one has always known but hitherto has failed to adequately acknowledge. It is a way of embracing a faith we already naturally possess, but in fitting in with the expectations of others we had somehow misplaced.

The same year Merton became Master of Scholastics he also composed one of his most famous prayers of spiritual yearning and self-abnegation:

> My Lord God, I have no idea where I am going. I do not see the road ahead of me. I cannot know for certain where it will end. Nor do I really know myself, and the fact that I think I am following your will does not mean that I am actually doing it. But I believe the desire to please does in fact please you. And I hope I have that desire in all that I am doing. I hope that I will never do anything apart from that desire. And I know that if I do this you will lead me by the right road though I may know nothing about it. Therefore will I trust you always though I may know nothing about it. Therefore will I trust you always though I may seem to be lost and in the shadow of death. I will not fear, for you are ever with me, and you will never leave me to face my fears alone.
> (*TIS*, p. 79)

Questions for reflection and discussion

1 Do you know where you are going? Is that a good thing? Why is this a more difficult question than one might suppose?
2 Merton noted that the primary 'problem' for the novices was 'thoughts'. What did he mean by that? Is this also true for those of us not living in monasteries?
3 What does it mean to 'live in ambiguity'? Why is this not the same thing as living with anxiety?

14

On Fourth and Walnut

A saint is not someone who has achieved a high degree of
sanctity but rather someone who has the ability to perceive
the sanctity in everybody else.
(Thomas Merton, *NS*)

In 1958 Merton underwent what some have described as a 'second
conversion experience'. While walking in the shopping district of
Louisville, Kentucky, he suddenly saw through the illusion of a
separate, holy life apart from the lives of others. According to his
own account, standing on the corner, he suddenly experienced a
oneness with all the shoppers around him that burst through all the
old dualisms separating sacred from secular, world from monk. He
realized then that if as a Trappist contemplative he had taken the
road less travelled into the soul's undiscovered country, he had not
escaped his humanity; he had merely taken the long way home. If
his monastic 'turn' had made him a 'new man' in Christ, he now saw
that that 'new man' was an ordinary person, and that the essence of
monasticism was not to be found in an aloofness from the world
but rather in compassion for it and identification with it. He writes:

In Louisville, at the corner of Fourth and Walnut, in the center
of the shopping district, I was suddenly overwhelmed with the
realization that I loved all those people, that they were mine
and I theirs, that we could not be alien to one another even
though we were total strangers. It was like waking from a
dream of separateness, of spurious self-isolation in a special
world, the world of renunciation and supposed holiness. The
whole illusion of a separate holy existence is a dream. Not that
I question the reality of my vocation, or of my monastic life:

but the conception of 'separation from the world' that we have in the monastery too easily presents itself as a complete illusion: the illusion that by making vows we become a different species of being, pseudo-angels, 'spiritual men', men of interior life, what have you . . . Thank God, thank God that I *am* like other men, that I am only a man among others.
(*CGB*, pp. 140–1)

Here Merton exposes the elitism that shadowed many of his earlier books and essays. Monks are not superior to ordinary people, but through a life devoted to prayer and reflection, they can become supremely common, connected and more truly themselves than those caught up in worldly illusions allow themselves to be. But there are spiritual illusions that clerics themselves are prone to – a different kind of spiritual pride. At Fourth and Walnut Merton found and confronted this common vocational hazard.

In the Prologue to *No Man is an Island* (1955), Merton quotes Amos 7.14: 'I am not a prophet, nor am I the son of a prophet, but I am a herdsman, plucking wild figs.' 'For it seems to me', Merton adds, 'that the first responsibility of a man of faith is to make his faith really a part of his life, not by rationalizing it but by living it' (*NM*, p. xiv).

Questions for reflection and discussion

1 Do you think of yourself as an 'ordinary person'? Or are you really quite 'special'? Both? Neither?
2 Does it bother you to think that God loves your neighbours with all their flaws and faults as much as he loves you? Does it bother you to think that God loves your enemy (or rival) just as much as he loves you? What does this say about God? About you?
3 What did Merton wake up from (or wake up to?) at Fourth and Walnut?

15

Apology to an unbeliever

Believing means liberating the indestructible element in oneself, or, more accurately, being indestructible, or, more accurately, being.

Franz Kafka, *The Blue Octavo Notebooks*

For Thomas Merton the religious problem of the twentieth century was not only a problem of the growing number of unbelievers and atheists. It was also a problem of 'believers' who had substituted comfortable, cultural illusions and 'cheap grace' for authentic discipleship.[1] The faith that has grown cold, he pointed out, was not only the faith the unbeliever has lost, but the sentimental, false 'faith' the 'believer' has 'kept'.

We don't have to choose between faith and science, Merton argues, nor between Christ and the world. In fact, we can only choose Christ by choosing the world because that world is in him and encountered by us in the ground of our very own personal freedom. God is not an object, a thing, or '*Grande Dame*', but being itself – one with the ground of each of us. 'Atheists' exist in God, just as much as Christians do; they just do not call the ground of their being God – if they call it anything at all. This is where the dialogue can begin.

In *The Seven Storey Mountain*, Merton tells us:

Faith means doubt. Faith is not the suppression of doubt. It is the overcoming of doubt, and you overcome doubt by going through it. The man of faith who has never experienced doubt is not a man of faith. Consequently, the monk is the one who has to struggle in the depths of his being with the presence of doubt and to go through what some religions call the Great

Doubt, to break through beyond doubt into a servitude which
is very, very deep because it is not his own personal servitude,
it is the servitude of God himself, in us.
(*SSM*, p. 228)

In 1966, Merton published an essay addressed to 'unbelievers',
apologizing for the inadequacy and impertinence that had been
inflicted upon them in the name of religion. 'Faith comes by
hearing, says St. Paul, but by hearing what?' Merton asks.

The cries of snake-handlers? The soothing platitudes of the
religious operator? One must be able to listen to the inscru-
table ground of (one's) own being, and who am I to say that
[the atheists'] reservations about religious commitment do
not protect, in [them], this kind of listening?
(*FAV*, p. 210)

He goes on: 'While I certainly believe that the message of the Gospel
is something that we are called upon to preach, I think we will communicate it more intelligently in dialogue (p. 212).

I am reminded here of a question once posed to Gregory Boyle,
founder of Homeboys Industries, a street mission in East Los
Angeles. When asked when he brings up God in his ministry to
gang members, Boyle replied, 'Both immediately and never at all.'
That is to say, God is present in all his encounters with the homies,
but as to evangelical polemics? Never at all.

Besides, as Merton reminds us, 'Many who consider themselves
atheists are in fact persons who are discontented with the naïve idea
of God which makes him appear to be an "object" or a "thing" in
a merely finite and human sense.' 'Those who are familiar with the
apophatic tradition', he goes on to point out, 'are fully aware that
the inability to imagine God or to "experience" him as present, or
even to find him credible, is not something discovered by modern
man or confined to our own age' (*CIWA*, p. 168). The literature of
the mystics is filled with such dialogues, and the life of the Christian
contemplative is not a life of wilful concentration upon a few clear

and comforting ideas, but a life of inner struggle in which the believer, like Christ in the desert, is tested.

In fact, the well-known atheist Sam Harris, in the last half of his book *The End of Faith: Religion, Terror, and the Future of Reason*, acknowledges the possibility of an agnostic 'spirituality' that takes religious experience seriously as a form of a *secular phenomenology*. And the German philosopher Peter Sloterdijk calls all efforts to live in harmony with the cosmos – both sacred and secular – 'anthropo-technics' (his new, wider, more inclusive word for all those efforts, faiths and self-transcending practices currently lumped within the single term 'religion').[2]

But in the years following Merton's death – the late 1970s and 1980s – religious fundamentalists of several faith traditions launched an offensive against secular society, science and atheism. Their primary weapon was a rigid, reductive, scriptural literalism delivered with a rancorous righteousness. Their passionate, doctrinal rigidity ultimately gave birth to a backlash of militant atheisms at the turn of the last century. Figures such as Sam Harris, Christopher Hitchens and Richard Dawkins all published bestselling polemics. Yet few, if any, of these writers even acknowledged the apophatic tradition – if, in fact, they had ever heard of it at all.

The combative tenor of these books was in part a response to the onslaught of 20-plus years of pop apologetics that polarized and 'dumbed down' the public conversation concerning faith. I suspect Merton – had he been alive – would have no doubt agreed with much of what these atheists had to say, and yet still pointed out where many of them fall prey to the straw-man fallacy. The God they do not believe in is not a God Merton ever believed in, and the 'believers' they attack are often attention-seekers who use religion as a drug to sooth their anxieties or a club to beat those who disagree with them. Rational men and women of faith, Merton argued, do not reject science, secular wisdom or open dialogue. In fact, such things are the very fruits of faith – not its antitheses.

'What [the Christian contemplative] learns', Merton explains, 'is not a clearer idea of God but a deeper trust, a purer love and a more complete abandonment to the One he knows to be beyond all understanding' (*CIWA*, p. 163.) Yet in this 'abandonment', the contemplative has access to certain existential values which the contemporary atheist tends to forget, underestimate or ignore.

Admittedly, the apophatic experience of God as *unknowable* does, to some extent, verify the atheist's view that God is not an object of precise knowledge and so consequently cannot be apprehended as a thing to be studied. But the difference between the apophatic contemplative and the atheist is that, whereas the atheist's experience of God is purely negative, the faith of the contemplative is, as Merton puts it, 'negatively *positive*'. That is to say, the believer responds to his or her own cognitive limitations with humility and faith; whereas the non-believer – confronted with the limits of the mind – redoubles his or her calculative ambitions. It is almost as if the apophatic believer is more sceptical than the sceptic in that he or she suspects concepts per se, relinquishing any attempt to grasp God in any analogical or metaphorical terms.

This is not as much of an evasion as one might at first think, but rather a call for a shift away from a methodology of doubt to a 'rhetoric of assent'.[3] Rather than questioning *reality*, the first step is to question the notions upon which the doubting Cartesian ego holds forth. If the sceptic fails to take this move seriously, or the 'believer' refuses to acknowledge the sceptic's alternative 'faith' in doubt, the dialogue is over and the polemics ensue.

When Merton wrote his 'Apology to an Unbeliever' in 1966, he thought it was time for the Christian consciousness of God to be expressed in apophatic language. The medieval ideas of God formed in accord with medieval ideas about the cosmos, earth, physics, and the biological and psychological structure of humanity were clearly out of date, but, as he puts it, the 'reality of experience beyond concepts, however, [was] not itself modified by changes of culture' (*FAV*, p. 172).

By focusing on the phenomenological *experience of being*, Jesus is revealed as a living, inclusive, existential Messiah – not a cipher in our ever-changing cosmological constructs. And with that, faith is no longer an 'embracing of superstition' but a healthy recognition of the mystery within which both our language and our minds must humbly comply.

'If the deepest ground of our being is love,' Merton writes, 'then in that very love itself and nowhere else will I find myself, and the world, and my brother, and Christ. It is not a question of either/or but all-in-one' (*FAV*, pp. 155–6).

So, in the end, Merton agrees with those atheists who deny God's existence as some sort of super concept, or 'thing', but he would disagree with those who then draw the conclusion that God, therefore, does not exist. What does not exist is the Cartesian God-object. What does exist is Being – revealed in and through the love that rises in us out of that which is beyond us.

Merton explained:

My own peculiar task in my Church and in my world has been that of the solitary explorer who, instead of jumping on all the latest bandwagons at once, is bound to search the existential depths of faith in its silences, its ambiguities, and in those certainties which lie deeper than the bottom of anxiety. In these depths there are no easy answers, no pat solutions to anything. It is a kind of submarine life in which faith sometimes mysteriously takes on the aspect of doubt when, in fact, one has to doubt and reject conventional surrogates that have taken the place of faith. On this level, the division between Believer and Unbeliever ceases to be so crystal clear.
(*FAV*, p. 213)

He concludes with this optimistic note, which unfortunately has yet to come true.

The most hopeful sign of religious renewal is the authentic sincerity and openness with which some Believers are beginning to recognize this (need for the faithful to doubt cheap grace and pop theology). At the very moment when they had to gather for a fanatical last-ditch stand, these Believers are dropping their defensiveness, their defiance, and their

mistrust. They are realizing that a faith that is afraid of other people is not faith at all. A faith that supports itself by condemning others is itself condemned by the Gospel.
(*FAV*, pp. 213–14)

As the poet Rilke says, 'we fling our emptiness out of our arms into the spaces we breathe so that the birds might feel the expanded air with more passionate flying'.[4]

This courageous self-giving – open to believer and unbeliever alike – represents the new metaphysical dispensation emerging on the far side of the modernist divide between atheism and theism. This is where every practising contemplative, mystic and true scientist labours and has always laboured. And now that the sceptics have vented some of their resentments and the 'magic' Christians have had their fundamentalist say, perhaps a real conversation as to our role in this cosmos can begin – free from invective, straw-men arguments and polemical grandstanding.

I'd like to close with two paragraphs taken from a letter Merton wrote a year after his 'apology' appeared in the *Harper's Magazine* (1966).

God is not a 'problem' and we who live the contemplative life have learned by experience that one cannot know God as long as one seeks to solve 'the problem of God.' To seek to solve the problem of God is to seek to see one's own eyes. One cannot see one's own eyes because they are that which sees and God is the light by which we see – by which we see not a clearly defined 'object' called God, but everything else in the invisible One. God is then the Seer and the seeing, but on earth He is not seen.
(*HGL*, p. 157)

And yet, Merton's more telling point follows:

But the language of Christianity – has been so used and so misused that sometimes you distrust it: you do not know whether or not behind the word 'cross' there stands the experience of mercy and salvation, or only the threat of punishment. If my word means anything to you, I can say to you that I have experienced the cross to mean mercy and not cruelty, truth and not deception; that the news of the truth and love of Jesus is the true good news, but in our time it speaks out in strange places. And perhaps it speaks out in you more than it does in me; perhaps Christ is nearer to you than he is to me.

This I say without shame or guilt because I have learned to rejoice that Jesus is in the world in people who know Him not, that He is at work in them when they think themselves far from Him, and it is my joy to tell you to hope though you think that for you of all [people] hope is impossible. *Hope not because you think you can be good, but because God loves us irrespective of our merits and whatever is good in us comes from His love, not from our own doing.* Hope because Jesus is with those who are poor and outcast and perhaps despised even by those who should seek them and care for them more lovingly because they act in God's name . . . No one on earth has reason to despair of Jesus, because Jesus loves [people], loves [them] in [their] sin, and we too must love [people] in [their] sin. (*HGL*, pp. 156–7; italics mine)

Questions for reflection and discussion

1 What is it that 'unbelievers' believe that the 'believers' don't? And what is it that 'believers' don't believe that 'unbelievers' believe? (You might need to make a little chart to sort this out.) What have you discovered?

2 What does Merton mean when he says that 'faith sometimes mysteriously takes on the aspect of doubt when one has to reject the conventional surrogates that have taken the place of faith'? What conventional 'surrogates' to faith is he talking about?

16

'The Root of War is Fear'

Not to predict, but to seize upon reality in its moment of highest expectation and tension toward the new.
(Thomas Merton, *LE*)

Merton's entry into politics began in 1961 with the publication of his poem 'Original Child Bomb', a satirical anti-poem about the atomic bombing of Hiroshima, and his poem 'Chants to be Used in Processions around a Site with Furnaces', another satirical anti-poem describing the thoughts of a Nazi Concentration Camp commandant ('I made improvements!'). From then until the end of his life, Merton continued to offer his views on the crises of his time, from the Cold War to the Civil Rights Movement to the Vietnam War.

The best single description of Merton's involvement in the peace movement comes from Jim Forest, a Catholic Worker and Vietnam War protester:

Merton was the Parish Priest of the Catholic Peace Movement, for as an ordained monk under vows of obedience, Merton did not participate in any anti-war demonstrations or acts of civil disobedience – like Dorothy Day or Dan and Phil Berrigan – but in writing essays for *The Catholic Worker* Newspaper and engaging in personal correspondence with Catholic war protestors, conscientious objectors, and the leaders of the Catholic anti-war movement.

Merton was someone to whom you could go to confession, who could give you advice about your vocation, who might be able to tell you where you were missing the boat, what you might be doing, and get you back in line again.[1]

One of Merton's most influential essays from this period in his life was 'The Root of War is Fear', where he laid out the psychological and spiritual origins of hate, political violence and social discord.

Reading that essay today, one is struck by how contemporary it seems and how useful Merton's ethical insights remain as a guide against nurturing resentments or projecting one's unconscious biases and stereotypes on to other people. Such ethical blindness born of a certain laziness of mind falls in line with what Milan Kundera has called 'the non-thought of received ideas', the bad habit of confusing 'labels' with actualities, and pejorative 'nicknames' for the complex people they are designed to defame.

But Merton thinks the roots of war go even deeper than this. 'At the root of all war', he tells us, 'is fear: not so much the fear men have of one another as they have of *everything*. It is not merely that they do not trust one another; they do not even trust themselves' (1 John 4.20–21). If one is not sure when or if someone else may try to kill us, we also aren't sure when and if we might turn around and kill ourselves. 'We cannot trust, anything', he sums up, 'because we have ceased to believe in God' (*MR*, p. 276).

This may strike some readers as a bit of a non sequitur, but Merton sees the militarization of the world – particularly in the case of the Cold War and the nuclear arms race – as having its origin in the lying and posturing of our frightened false selves.

It isn't our hatred of others, he tells us, so much as our unconscious hatred and doubts about ourselves – 'too deep and powerful to face' – that make us see our own evil in others because we refuse to see it in ourselves. Rage, shame and guilt are projected outwards, so when we see crime in others we treat it just as we treat it in ourselves: we 'correct' it by killing it or putting it out of our sight as quickly as possible. Rather than accepting human imperfections with compassion, humility and identification, we banish them from our lives, either by destroying them, ignoring them or locking them away. This is the psychological meaning of Christ's observation, 'What you have done to the least of these, you have done to me' (Matthew 25.40–45, author's paraphrase).

We don't see this because we interpret our own immoral acts

as necessary evils or 'involuntary mistakes' (even sometimes as originating in the 'crimes' of our victims). So, when others hold us responsible for our behaviour, that blame becomes just another reason for us to hate them more and seek their elimination more vociferously.

We try to dismiss our own faults by noticing worse failings in other people. 'Hence I minimize my own sins and compensate for doing so by exaggerating the faults of others' (*MR*, p. 277).

All this is mostly done unconsciously, of course, as René Girard has pointed out. 'This kind of fictional thinking', Merton says, 'is especially dangerous when it is supported by a whole elaborate pseudo-scientific structure of myths' (*MR*, p. 277). Substitute 'conspiracy theories' for 'myth' and you have a pretty good description of how contemporary politics functions and donor money is raised.

To paraphrase Merton, when the world is in a state of moral confusion and denial, and everyone is running away from responsibility, blame and moral accountability, 'we expend all our efforts in constructing more fictions with which to account for our ethical failures' (*NS*, p. 114). In a world rife with such recrimination, 'the good will of negotiators looks increasingly pathetic – and they find themselves reviled, blamed and treated with contempt, destroyed as victims of the universal self-hate projected upon them' (*NS*, p. 115).

Thus it is, Merton explains, that we never see the one truth that would solve our ethical and political problems: that we are *all* more or less wrong, that we are *all* at fault, *all* limited and obstructed by our mixed motives, self-deception, greed, self-righteousness, aggression and hypocrisy (1 Peter 5.6).

If we can accept the inevitably 'limited' good intentions of others and work with them any way we can, we strike a blow against our own unconscious malice, intolerance, lack of realism, and ethical and political quackery.

Perhaps in the end the first step towards peace must be a realistic acceptance of the fact that our political ideals are to a great extent illusions, fictions to which we cling out of motives

that are not always perfectly honest. And this self-deception prevents us from seeing any good or any practicality in the behaviour of our rivals, 'which may, of course, be in many ways even more illusory and dishonest than our own'. This is why we must work together 'doggedly' and hope in the little good that may yet be found.
(*MR*, pp. 278–9; see Matthew 5.44)

Two things are worth noting here. Merton's idea that (1) political realism requires us to build our compromises on the solid ground of self-knowledge and the acknowledgement of human limitations, not upon over-simplifications, utopian ideals or fear. And (2) that we must learn that the art of peace-making is an art of humility, fortitude and unflinching honesty (not a job for the impatient, the insecure or the professional 'strategist').

This is as true for the peace in our homes as it is for the peace between nations.

Merton's analysis in 'The Root of War is Fear' is further elaborated in his 'Letter to a White Liberal', where he explains why Black civil rights advocates are right to distrust the support of White liberals who do not truly understand how deeply White supremacy resides in the very foundations of American civilization. And that it is not enough to simply applaud reforms that do away with obvious injustices – segregated schools and buses – without looking at where those injustices come from in the first place, namely the belief that race is a marker of human attributes. Race, Merton reminds us, is a cultural construct – a myth White people have profited from whether they know it or not – what Merton has pointed out as the lie behind the fear.

Merton believed that the Civil Rights Movement, in its deepest and most spiritual dimensions, could awaken the conscience of the White man to the reality of his amorality and sin (however unconscious and habitual), so that he would be able to see that the Black problem is really a White problem and that the cancer eating away at American democracy is 'only partly manifested in racial segregation with all its consequences, (but primarily) rooted in the heart of the Whiteman himself' (*SD*, pp. 45–6).

His solution lies inherent in his diagnosis. 'The message of the Christian is not that "the kingdom might come, that peace might be established, but that the kingdom is come, and that there will be peace for those who seek it"' (*SD*, p. 188). For the Christian, justice is not sought because it is a key to socio-economic progress; it is sought because the salvation of our souls depends upon it 'right now' in this world (not the next). Truth, beauty and justice is where the world finds its perfection in the present. The victory has already been won (we just haven't realized it yet).

Questions for reflection and discussion

1 Have you ever been stereotyped, labelled or treated as an outsider? What was that like? How did you respond to such treatment?
2 If 'the root of war' is fear, what is the root of fear?
3 Have you ever hated someone? What fanned the flames of this affliction? How did it pass? Or did it?

17

Re-opening the Bible

The central content of the Bible, what the Bible is really about, what opens itself to the amazed understanding to one who really grasps the essential message is this unique claim: that the inner truth of man and of human existence is revealed in a certain kind of event. This event has the nature of Kairos, crisis, or judgment. Challenged by a direct historical inter-vention by God (which may be doubtful and obscure but is nonetheless decisive), man may respond with the engagement of his deepest freedom, or he can evade the encounter by various specious excuses.
(Thomas Merton, *OTB*)

Merton's fallible, paradoxical life ended abruptly by accidental electrocution while attending a monastic conference in Bangkok in December 1968. The exact cause of his death remains unknown because his body was found after the fact, alone in his room with a 'shorted' direct-current electric fan resting on his chest. No autopsy was ever performed. The evidence suggests accidental electrocution (or heart attack). Conclusive evidence for any of these explanations is not definitive. He was 53 years old.

When he died, Merton was at yet another crossroads in his life. His interest in Tibetan Buddhism was just beginning, as were his travels outside the monastery. He was considering moving to a more private 'Western' hermitage, reading Fanon, Foucault, Barthes, Mary Daly and the liberation theologians, and writing about Ishi, non-violence, and the Black revolution. His scheduled retreat with the Revd Martin Luther King was cancelled due to King's assassin-ation in April. Robert F. Kennedy was arranging for Merton to speak at the White House but that also had to be cancelled due to Robert Kennedy's assassination a month later. Merton died in December of that same year – 1968.

And yet Merton's disturbingly sudden death was followed by a second life in books. Decades worth of unpublished writings, letters and journals all found their way into print over the next 50 years – twice as many volumes as he ever published in his lifetime. These works – including most of his personal letters and private journals – addressed nearly every topic of interest and concern in his time, from the dilemmas of inter-faith dialogue to the efficacy of non-violent activism, to the pros and cons of liberation theology, feminism, monastic renewal, the Black revolution, multiculturalism, White fragility, contemplative prayer, meditation, Eastern Orthodoxy, Sufism, Buddhism, Native American spirituality, and even death-of-God a-theologies.

One of Thomas Merton's last essays was an introduction to the Time-Life Bible. The Time-Life Bible itself was never completed, but Merton's 85-page introduction was published as a book in 1970 under the title *Opening the Bible*. Unlike Merton's other writings on biblical texts and themes, this introduction presented an overview of the entire Bible as a vision of spiritual transformation and human liberation.

For Merton, the Bible's value did not derive primarily from its literary worth, although many sublime passages are contained within its pages. Nor did it derive from any explicit ideas, concepts or theories it contains, though there are plenty of those things too. Its value derives from its capacity to show us the possibility for redemption in our lives and then enact it within us.

The converted who are in solidarity with those who suffer the pain of the world are better prepared to read the Bible with the right pair of eyes. But many Bible readers are alienated from the book either by their affluence or by their assumption that it is a historical text about 'other people' in 'other times', or that it assumes a supernatural view of the world they believe themselves incapable of embracing. Or that the Bible's serial construction and internal contradictions demand from them a historical knowledge they simply do not possess.

For Merton, each of these objections misses the point entirely, for – as he tells us in this introduction – the Bible must be read *existentially.* That is to say, in order to read the Bible at all is to read it as if one's life depended on it, not as if the book were meant for someone else. The book's meaning and value simply does not yield itself to a purely analytical or dispassionate reading. An 'alienated reading', as Merton calls it, looks at the Bible as an artefact of the past or a species of antique theology. Neither reading is in sync with the book's true organizing principle.

An existential reading is like a devotional reading in that events, actions and conversations begin to take on larger meanings related to our own lives, bringing us into a direct relationship with 'an ultimate freedom which is at once ground and source of man's being, the center of his history and guide of his destinies' (*OTB*, p. 15). And because the Bible is centred on events and not concepts or theories, it addresses the whole human person, not just our critical faculties and intellects.

Furthermore, the events the Bible narrates are, for the most part, like Joycean 'epiphanies', 'breakthroughs' that shatter old limits and challenge us to a more inclusive, less rigid, sense of what it means to live a dedicated, responsible life.

The Bible presents us with a view of humanity as a tapestry of interwoven individual destinies blessed by covenants 'in which the law is fulfilled by emancipation from the law'.[1] And concludes with love, grace and fulfilment flowing from the self-emptying of Christ (kenosis), who models for us what it means to empty ourselves so as to be filled with grace through the power of Holy Spirit – thereby taking our place within the community of saints (Philippians 2.7).

The great temptation, Merton warns, is to settle for a superficial reading (and self) that affirms its own unity 'by shutting out other persons and by closing off the deepest area of inner freedom where the ego is no longer in conscious control' (*OTB*, p. 72). The power of God's word is that it can 'break through this comfortable little system and shatter all its precious selfish values, challenging us to risk a higher and more fundamental freedom' (*OTB*, p. 73).

In other words, to read the Bible *existentially* is to allow oneself to be challenged by its call to acts of justice and mercy, which changes our relationship to ourselves, God and other people. This is not just an initiation into a particular set of metaphysical beliefs or tribal rituals, as the experience of the text makes clear.

In other words, to read so existentially is to face our own contingency, radical need and personal insufficiency by identifying with the lives of the protagonists and antagonists whose lives and tragic destinies play out in bold, amoral relief. The difficulties the Bible presents us with are our difficulties. We are Noah and we are Esther, the prodigal son and the woman at the well. Only an alienated reader could think otherwise, preoccupied with 'the fact' that they themselves are somebody else rather than engaging with the events in the text as if they were their very own.

In his Pulitzer Prize-winning book *The Denial of Death*, Ernest Becker sees Kierkegaard making the same case for an existential Christianity that Merton does:

> The problem with conventional faith for Kierkegaard is that it can serve as a barrier to one's confrontation with pure possibility and so substitutes itself for the spiritual rebirth necessary for true Christian faith. We must first break through the bonds of our own given cultural heroic in order to be open to the true self. By so doing, we link the secret inner self, our authentic talent, our deepest feelings of uniqueness, our inner yearning for absolute significance, to the very ground of creation. Out of the ruins of the broken cultural persona there remains the mystery of the private, invisible, inner self which yearns for ultimate significance and cosmic heroism. This invisible mystery at the heart of every creature now attains its cosmic significance by affirming its connection with the invisible mystery at the heart of creation. This is the meaning of faith. At the same time, it is the merger of psychology and religion.[2]

Merton, perhaps, wouldn't describe faith as 'the merger of psychology and religion' so much as the merger of body with spirit, head with heart, and the human with God.

Questions for reflection and discussion

1 'Merton's gift to me, and countless others, was to share his way to rest in God and the abundant joy that goes with it' (Michael Cassagram ocso[3]). What, if anything, has been Merton's gift to you?

2 Does it seem wise (or merely futile) that, as T. S. Eliot suggests, all our seeking returns us to our beginnings in a way that we may know that place as if for the first time? What do we find out that we don't already know when we arrive back at our beginnings?

3 In what sense can it be said that the Bible 'reads us' as much as we read the Bible?

18

Life without care

> Be content. We are the body of Christ. We have found Him. He has found us. We are in him. He is in us. *There is nothing further to look for except the deepening of this life we already possess.* (Thomas Merton, *SS*)

There were days at the polytechnic after I taught some great writer like Dostoevsky or Whitman when I would feel such a sense of failure that I could barely walk back to my office. I was awash with shame for having betrayed their genius

One day, after just such a class, I crossed paths with one of my faculty friends, a poet who taught general education classes like me. He asked me why the long face. And I blurted out everything – the looks on my students' bored, disinterested faces, the tone of my voice shifting from pleading to whining in despair.

He accepted my complaints for the griping it was, and told me rather bluntly, 'The problem is that you care.'

'Of course,' I said. 'I wouldn't be here if I didn't care!'

He told me that the sooner I got over 'caring' the happier I would be.

His remarks – indeed, his whole attitude – made little sense to me. It sounded like cynicism, but this fellow was no cynic. If anything, he was one of the most idealistic people I had ever met. So what gives with this cynical advice?

A few years later I heard a recording of Thomas Merton's lecture 'A Life without Care', in which he explained how and why we burden ourselves with 'cares' about our jobs, our lives, our families and our relationships – indeed, how and why we allow ourselves to be 'devoured by care', going over things in our minds, piling reflection on reflection until we are sick to our stomachs.

'This is care, see!' Merton exclaims:

And we are here in this monastery to get rid of it. And we get rid of it by going through it. Since God offers to take the care of our affairs upon himself, let us once and for all abandon them to his infinite wisdom that we may never more be occupied with anything but Him and his interests . . .

God asks us to live in such a way that he will do the thinking about us so that we don't have to think about ourselves. And as we get on in the spiritual life, we have to learn to do that with matters of virtue. Caussade says you should reach the point where you don't think of your own virtue at all – you just do what you do, and he disposes of the outcome.

This presupposes, of course, that you are practicing some virtues and leading a halfway decent life. This is not easy because we are all prone to worry about a lot of things, but if you are going to live the solitary life, you must learn how to forget yourself and simply enjoy it.

. . . We are living in a world that is absolutely transparent, and God is shining through it all the time. And this is not just a nice story – it is true. We maybe cannot see this, but if we abandon ourselves to Him, we see it sometimes . . .

And what is it that makes the world opaque? It's 'care!' Because everything becomes opaque in so far as we regard it as individual objects. We become concerned with them and fail to see God – that is to say, the larger – infinite inter-connected forces at play. [Our lives] become *this* particular problem or thing – *this* day I have to live through – *this* job or challenge I have – *this* particular requirement or person . . . It comes to me as 'Something wrong here' in a big opaque package, and I spend my time opening it up. But after the event or when we come to know the disreputable person or challenge, we find there is nothing there . . .

People are transparent manifestations of the humanity of God – and redeemed in Christ. This does not become apparent so long as we attempt to love the world only for itself. [1]

To apply Merton's perspective to my own teaching problems born of 'care', it appears I was looking at my students and my uninspired 'teaching' as opaque individual problems in an unredeemed world. In short, I was taking them and myself out of their holy 'perfection' and reframing them as objects in need of my 'care'. Taken in by my own projections, I had lost my ability to 'let things in', giving a moral meaning and metaphysical reality to the 'things' I 'cared' about. That is what it means to 'care' too much – it is a way of 'knowing better' or, perhaps more accurately said, 'a way of distrusting God'.

Merton quotes Caussade: 'Self abandonment is the continual forgetfulness of self which leaves the soul free to eternally love God and untroubled by those fears, reflections, and regrets and anxieties which the care of one's own perfection and salvation gives.'[2]

Questions for discussion and reflection

1 So what do you think? Does Merton have a point? Or is he just suggesting that we stop caring about things?
2 Do you store your treasures on earth? Is that where your heart is? If not, where is it?
3 If all of the things we strive for are impermanent, and life is more than food and the body more than clothes, what then are we? And what are our lives for?

19

The Merton legacy

If anyone thinks it appropriate that I leave an epitaph as a mark or monument of evidence of my having been here (for some reason or purpose), and as testimony of some contribution made to the world . . . then let it be this: 'Go out without leaving a trace.'
(Attributed to Thomas Merton[1])

In a word, the work Christ does in the world, through the action of His Spirit, through His Church, and through His holy sacraments, is the work of incorporating and transforming us into Himself.
(Thomas Merton, *LB*)

Thomas Merton was an outsider who defined himself in opposition to the world in both word and deed, and then discovered a way back into dialogue with it and compassion for it. He was the herald of a still yet to be realized contemplative counter-culture, offering us a vision of the interior life free from rigid philosophical categories, narrow political agenda, and trite religious truisms.

Despite Merton's reputation as a 'spiritual master' and mystic, there was something about him that was 'familiar'. He spoke like we do. His experiences were often common, his expressions candid and sincere. And when we read his books and essays, we find ourselves in the presence of someone like ourselves, a normal person, someone we think we could talk to who seems capable of understanding our point of view.

And yet his voice also carries a certain intellectual urgency. He's so busy being born that he wants to talk about how it's going, what he's discovered, how far he has got and where he has faced detours, setbacks and U-turns. That he became a monk lends credibility to the seriousness of his search and gravitas to his reflections. And the fact that he never turned into a television evangelist, radio personality or dogmatic theologian, charismatic retreat master or celebrity guru, preserved in him the childlike innocence of a beginner.

He was never above starting over – returning to the origins of his faith, the roots of religion itself, or even to personal metaphysical intuitions and longings. As a result, he rediscovered himself again and again in dialogue with many different spiritual teachers and traditions, transforming his wrong turns and personal enthusiasms into provocative spiritual achievements

It is futile to systematize his systemless mind; absurd to gather Merton's many interests within a single theme. Besides, searching his writings for a unity they do not possess only diminishes them. Merton's Christian witness – an unending series of meditations on his experiences in solitude – cannot be understood simply in terms of the religious commonplaces it interrogates and often redefines. To try to detect its unity or ultimate organizing principle is to spoil its power as surprise and its 'absolutely, paradoxically placed teleological' nature. So, it seems most fitting to close this book of questions and provocations not with a conclusion but with more questions and prompts for further inquiry.

It is helpful to remember here that Merton never made a business of his writings or his reputation. He never had to. His royalties went to the order to which he pledged obedience. He didn't need 'capital'. He wasn't saving for retirement or running his own non-profit organization, managing a private school or directing a movement. This gave him another level of credibility and freedom, one not shared by his more socially 'engaged' and worldly ambitious peers.

If Merton never assumed the role of public intellectual, prophet, religious journalist, culture critic or saint, it was because he was something different, something rarer: a simple, honest man on a sincere spiritual quest who reported back to us candidly about what he had found – or failed to find – without pretence or duplicity.

Merton, as noted, never referred to himself as a 'spiritual master' or even as a 'success'. He declined a nomination to run for abbot at Gethsemani, joking that the only reason he could imagine for anyone nominating him was as a ruse to somehow increase their beer allotment. He was never interested in making his way up the hierarchy. He wouldn't have known what to do if he had. He preferred the titles 'marginal man' and 'ordinary person'. Or, as he put it after his revelation on the corner of Fourth and Walnut, 'simply a man among others'.

'Man is more glorified', he told us, 'by [someone] who uses the good things of this life in simplicity and with gratitude than by the nervous asceticism of someone who is agitated about every detail of his self-denial' (*NM*, pp. 114–15).

Notwithstanding Merton's reputation as a 'world-famous hermit' celebrated by Pope Francis in a speech delivered before both houses of Congress in the USA, Merton remains for us a brilliant, if sometimes controversial, spiritual friend whose humanity and candour, almost as much as his devotion to Christ, can still touch our hearts and educate our conscience.

Merton wrote from his heart not just his head – and felt things forwards rather than simply planned them out. His work proceeds less like a series of arguments and more like a gallery of paintings, each unfolding organically in relationship to some mysterious absolute contained within them that he was trying to ferret out and disclose. Rather than laying down the law, Merton followed the contours and consequences of ideas and values, inviting his readers to enflesh them by adding their own elaborations and intuitions to the issue at hand.

When asked if he thought Thomas Merton would ever be canonized, Merton's former abbot Flavian Burns replied:

I think Merton's idea of a saint was a person who was completely aware of his need for God's mercy, a person with the self-knowledge that you don't become a saint on your own. God makes you a saint. That you have to be willing to let Him do it and own up to your own poverty. And according to that definition of a saint, I think he was a saint. He was a person very conscious of his need for God's mercy, his sinfulness, his weakness. And I don't think he was in for any surprises when he came before the Lord on Judgment Day.[2]

As a writer, Merton, like James Joyce, was attempting 'to wake up from the nightmare of history'. Joyce had taught him that a writer brings their whole life into dialogue with experience – and this included examining one's flaws, faults, temporality, context and ever-present mortality. And like Joyce, Merton – despite being a devout Catholic – never thought of himself as an institutional spokesman. Or rather, though Merton spoke as a monk living in a Cistercian monastery committed to a Christian contemplative calling, it was always as an apostle-in-progress that he spoke to us, linking doctrines to personal experience and personal experience to Scripture as he proceeded, raising questions along the way, questions that had not yet been posed (and so not answered) by authorities, peers or even himself.

Partiality, error, imperfection, mortality and human limitations were baked into his inquiries and made up the fits and starts of his admittedly 'human' search for God. All of which is served up to us as food for thought – and direct confirmation of every metaphysical longing within us. For sooner or later we all arrive at what Merton called 'that virginal point', the absolute nothingness at the centre of our minds, which all too often remains a 'problem' to be solved or a 'mystery' to be accepted when it is, in fact, neither of these things but the threshold of *pure consciousness* in which the subject as such "disappears"' (*Z&B*, pp. 23–4).

'The more I see of it,' Merton confessed, 'the more I realize the absolute primacy and necessity of silent, hidden, poor, apparently fruitless prayer' (*HGL*, p. 371). This was not a lament over God's seeming inaction in the face of injustice but a recognition of the only thing that has ever really worked in the long run has been infinite patience, unwavering faith and limitless love.

Spiritual writing, growing out of such desert experiences, demands a different sort of apprenticeship than does the priesthood or even the lay religious life, for, unlike public speaking and contrary to liturgical ritual, the writer constantly revisits and reviews previous beliefs, concepts and experiences in the light of ever-changing contexts and ever-deepening faith.

The emphasis here is not creating an alternative world in one's own imagination or applying doctrines to circumstances or even facts to values. The spiritual writer articulates what it means to live in a world created by God and shared with other God-created people. The spiritual writer is not the genius creator at the centre of his own metaphysical universe but something less outwardly spectacular and more inwardly lasting: a living witness to his own solitary soul's irrepressible, one-of-a-kind divine originality and ethical responsibilities.

The contemporary philosopher Slavoj Žižek once described a spiritual master as a 'vanishing mediator who gives you back to yourself', who delivers you to the abyss of your freedom. This opens your eyes to why being who you are is the same thing as being who you could be. Žižek says:

When we listen to a true leader, we discover what we want (or rather, what we always already wanted without knowing it). A Master is needed because we cannot accede to our freedom directly – to gain access we have to be pushed from outside, since our 'natural state' is one of inert hedonism.[3]

The paradox here is that 'the more we live as "free individuals with no Master," the more we are effectively non-free, caught within the existing frame of possibilities – we have to be impelled or disturbed into freedom by a Master'.[4] This is to say, we must first be awakened to the fact that we are not really the social animals we believe ourselves to be but rather something more, something absolutely other, made in the image of God.

In one of Merton's early drafts of *The Inner Experience*, he put it this way:

There is only one problem on which all my existence, my peace, my happiness depends: to discover myself in God. If I find him I will find myself and if I find my true self I will find Him.[5]

In his book *Silent Lamp: The Thomas Merton Story*, William H. Shannon notes that in the 1950s Catholicism had become an 'answer factory' churning out ideologically ordained positions on virtually any question or concern anyone might have. It became overly more concerned with having the right answers than with whether it was asking the right questions. 'Its aim was unbendingly apologetic and polemic. It needed to prove that Catholics were right and everybody else wrong.'[6] But in this fervour to meet the Cold War's challenge of competing ideologies and faiths, the Church had forgotten its prophetic role in reshaping the questions themselves and reframing the desires pursued by the post-war world at large.

Merton's commitment to the apophatic tradition of the Desert Fathers and Mothers changed all that. Through his articulate re-animation of his theology of questions, his interest in Zen and his studies of the apostolic Fathers and mystics of the Church, he revived the eschatological dimension of the Christian faith from the inside out – applying largely forgotten pre-modern spiritual assumptions, practices and techniques to contemporary problems, issues and concerns.

The poverty stricken, imprisoned, immigrants, homeless, addicted and otherwise marginalized have a natural empathy and sympathy for one another. They know something together that the rest of us do not really know at all. Baptism was once an initiation into that knowledge of solidarity with the poor, which in our bourgeois worlds no longer seems to exist in the same way (Romans 6.3–4).

Merton's message was not what Christians *must* or *ought to be*, but that Christians *can* be. Christians can open their minds to other religions and interrogate other traditions; they can think for themselves and sometimes even against themselves; they can interrogate the dogmas of modernism and postmodernism, explore ethical roads not taken, love their enemies, not just believe in God but experience his compassion moving within and through them, and find both wisdom and comfort in the hitherto marginalized contemplative traditions of the universal Church, seeing the teachings of the mystics with new eyes and praying for mercy with new confidence.

Today, more than ever, we need the witness of Thomas Merton – his way of living and his critique of modernity – and yet our access to it is more difficult than ever. Once misunderstood because he was too far ahead of his times, now he is undervalued because he spoke in the vernacular of religious existentialism. We could wait for a change in intellectual fashion to hear once again what his writings mean to our time, but who knows how long that might take and what tragedies could occur in the meantime. It is up to us now to fully embrace his contemplative prophecies.

Thomas Merton was a part of that intellectual cadre (which includes Gandhi, Solzhenitsyn, Thich Nat Hahn, Desmond Tutu, Edith Stein, Martin Luther King and others) who, in the middle of the last century, gave new life and meaning to the old verities. They embraced the post-war anti-colonial transvaluation of values that advocated for universal human rights, democracy, non-violence and religious pluralism – all in the hope of putting an end to intolerance, racism, sexism and the parochial prejudices of invidious hierarchical systems.

But in recent years we have seen a backlash against this perennial philosophy driven by nationalist and authoritarian movements. Pope Francis and the Dalai Lama have championed contemporary contemplative prophets like Merton, but we have to turn to fiction to help us revive some of the untapped potential of Merton's spiritual legacy.

The New Pope was a television series on HBO, written and directed by the Academy Award-winning Italian auteur and novelist Paolo Sorrentino. It's the sequel to his controversial HBO series *The Young Pope*, which aired in 2016. In *The Young Pope*, Sorrentino imagined what might happen if a youthful Gen X cardinal (played by Jude Law) ascended to the papacy. But his sequel to this series, *The New Pope*, took on a more ambitious literary project: to imagine a 'new' pope come of age in the last century, steeped in the perennial philosophy, who could, nevertheless, speak to several generations of abandoned spiritual seekers, defend the dispossessed and yet still serve as inspirational witness and practical counsellor to the members and ecclesiastical hierarchy of the universal Church.

It was a bold undertaking. So bold that its ambitious religious themes were lost on many ex-Catholic and non-Catholic television critics, who focused their reviews on the show's controversial sex scenes, glitzy sequences of nuns dancing to pop music, and creepy Vatican politicians, pretty much ignoring the seriousness of the religious ideas being advanced, ideas powerfully and poetically expressed by the charismatic New Pope, 'John Paul III', played by John Malkovich, a world-weary student and disciple of John Henry Newman.

Here is the New Pope's first address from the balcony on Vatican Square:

The girls who snubbed us. The boys who deserted us. The strangers who ignored us. The parents who misunderstood us. The employers who rejected us. The mentors who doubted us. The bullies who beat us. The siblings who mocked us. The friends who abandoned us. The conformists who excluded us. The kisses we were denied because no one saw us. They were all too busy turning their gaze elsewhere, while I was directing my gaze at you. Only at you. Because I am one of you.

Sorrow has no hierarchy. Suffering is not a sport. There is no final ranking. Tormented by acne and shyness, by stretch marks and discomfort, by baldness and insecurity, by anorexia and bulimia, by obesity and diversity, reviled for the color of our skin, our sexual orientation, our empty wallets, our physical impairments, our arguments with our elders, our inconsolable weeping, the abyss of our insignificance, the caverns of our lost, the emptiness inside us, the recurring incurable thought of ending it all, nowhere to rest, nowhere to stand, nothing to belong to. Nothing. Nothing. Nothing.

Yes, that is how we felt. And just like you, I remember it all. But it no longer matters, that the world took issue with us. For now, it is us who shall take issue with the world. We will no longer tolerate being named as a problem. Because in point of fact they are the problem, we are the solution. We who have been betrayed and abandoned, rejected and misunderstood, put aside and diminished. 'There is no place for you here', they

told us with their silence. 'Then where is our place?' we im-
plored them with our silence. We never received that reply.
But now we know, yes? We know our place. Our place is here.
Our place is the Church.

Cardinal Biffi said it first, and in an astonishing and simple
way: 'We are all miserable wretches whom God brought
together to form a glorious Church.' Yes, we are all miserable
wretches. Yes, we are all the same, and yes, we are the forgotten
ones, but no longer. From this day forth, we shall no longer be
forgotten, I assure you. They will remember us because we are
the Church . . .

That is who we are. We are a truth.'[7]

Here, in a nutshell, is Sorrentino's idea of what a fearless new pope
might, could and perhaps even *should* say. But for such a pope
to exist, first someone has to imagine him – just as Merton had to
imagine a contemporary contemplative Catholicism before it could
exist. Although, as we have seen, he never planned it that way.

Thomas Merton was many things – priest, poet, monk, mem-
oirist, novelist, homilist, contemplative, photographer, social critic,
theologian, cartoonist, teacher, mystic, spiritual director, corres-
pondent to world historical thinkers as well as ordinary people,
lay Catholics, religious and atheists. He was a student of Christian
mysticism, Zen, Sufism, Tibetan Buddhism, social anthropology,
philosophy, intellectual history and monasticism.

For Merton, ideas had weight and bore consequences both in
this world and the next. Ideas shaped societies, cultures, history,
the inner life and all of our relationships. They shape our experiences and define the difference between the so-called atheist and
so-called Christian.

As a writer, Merton shared in the modern artist's task of cor-
recting the perpetual misnaming of experience. His poetry, like
his prayers, reoriented our perceptions by decentring our egos and
revealing the value of things in God's greater design.

Christianity was, for Merton the convert, still coming into being
within him. He didn't think of his faith as 'finished' or as a set of

metaphysical axioms he 'believed' in nor as some abstract thing floating somewhere 'out there'. It was, for him, the very substance of his subjective reality. God present in his heart and mind, illuminating everything (including himself) from within.

Merton put it this way:

> We are trying to recognize God by forsaking ourselves to His will. His will, however, is not a simple matter of arbitrary decrees and laws external to us. It is the law of love laid in our own nature and in the revelation of spiritual love and personal freedom. The fruit of that love is the restoration of all things in Christ, the union of all beings with God, by means of man, by the exercise of the freedom of man.
> (TL, p. 2)

This was the same message Thomas Merton gave when he held a three-day retreat for Vietnam War protesters at Gethsemani in 1964 and asked the question, 'By what right do we protest?'

He didn't ask, 'How might we bring down the military industrial complex?' Or, 'What political tactics might best serve us in our goal to stop the war?' He asked, '*By what right* do we protest?' Which is another way of asking, 'What are we protecting?' What have we witnessed that demands our testimony and dissent?

Do we have the eyes to see what is actually before us? Have we awoken from our Cartesian slumber or are we still living in an alienated daze? Are we really seeing ourselves and our adversaries clearly? Are we protesting what we ourselves have become as well as what others have made us suffer? Are we aware of the unjust order that we ourselves have perpetuated through our tacit consent? By what right do we break our silence and, having broken it, by what right do we say the things we have to say? Is the underlying premise of our arguments true, honest, transformative, godly and healing?

In other words, he was asking for self-reflection as to how the war protesters had arrived at their dissent and what step they could take to re-enter history in a prophetic way. What seed had been planted in their lives that led them to disengage from one misspent set of social values for another. He was looking for a new way to perceive social sin and collective irresponsibility by reminding himself and his fellow dissidents that they needed to be healed.

Merton was asking the Vietnam War protestors to redefine themselves as neither victims nor executioners, neither comic nor tragic participants in history, but rather as tragic-comic witnesses to a suffering world armed with the believer's capacity to be humbled – and, thereby, changed.

'About all we have is a great need for roots,' he concluded, 'but to know this is already something.' We can collaborate, we can work together, we can remain united and focused and committed if we know the roots and the soil from which we and our protests come. This transforms the usual progressive political question as to what is to be done to the more important issue: what is it that unites us in our protest? Where do we come from? What do we stand for? Why are we so late to the party?

In *Raids on the Unspeakable* Merton warns his colleagues:

You are not big enough to accuse the whole age effectively but let us say you are in dissent. You are in no position to issue commands, but you can speak words of hope. Shall this be the substance of your message? Be human in this most inhuman of ages; guard the image of man for it is the image of God. You agree? Good. Then go with my blessing. But I warn you, do not expect to make many friends. As for the Unspeakable – his implacable presence will not be disturbed by a little fellow like you!
(*RU*, pp. 5–6)

The further we move away from Merton in time, the more we need his counsel and example. Let us close with his blessing for the present moment.

In a time of drastic change one can be too preoccupied with what is ending or too obsessed with what seems to be beginning. In either case one loses touch with the present and with its obscure but dynamic possibilities. What really matters is openness, readiness, attention, courage to face risk. You do not need to know precisely what is happening, or exactly where it is all going. In such an event, courage is the authentic form taken by love. What you need is to recognize the possibilities and challenges of the present moment, and to embrace them with courage, faith, and hope.[8]

Questions for discussion and reflection

1 Now that you've finished the book, reread the epigraph on the frontispiece. Does it mean the same thing to you now as when you first read it?
2 What does it mean to be a contemplative?
3 Has Merton's story deepened your awareness of your own need for God's mercy? Or taught you something different? What?

Notes

Introduction

1 Rowan Williams, *A Silent Action: Engagements with Thomas Merton* (Louisville, KY: Fons Vitae, 2011) p. 19.
2 From Paul Wilkes (ed.), *Merton: By Those Who Knew Him Best* (San Francisco, CA: Harper and Row, 1984), p. 111.

1 An apostle, not a genius

1 S. Kierkegaard, *The Present Age*, trans. Alexander Dru (San Francisco, CA: Harper and Row, 1962), p. 105.
   Teleology is the meaning of things in terms of the ultimate goal towards which they aspire. An 'immanent' teleology focuses on the material fulfilment of a potential form (a seed becomes a tree), whereas to be 'absolutely, paradoxically, teleologically placed' is to apprehend all things in terms of their participation in the fulfilment of everything else. A tree is the co-mingling of rain and earth and sunlight in what Merton calls 'the General Dance', whose ultimate end and consummate meaning is the meaning of all meanings.
2 Zen koans are a sophisticated system of self-inquiry utilizing riddles or puzzles, created more than a thousand years ago. They act as an unveiling medium so the spiritual student can receive a self-liberating revelation.

2 The *via negativa*

1 Richard Rohr, *Immortal Diamond* (San Francisco, CA: Jossey Bass, 2013), p. 25.
2 William Wordsworth, 'Ode: Intimations of Immortality from Recollections in Early Childhood', in *English Romantic Poetry*, ed. Stanley Appelbaum (Mineola, NY: Dover Publications, 1996).
3 Fernando Pessoa, *The Book of Disquiet*, ed. and trans. Richard Zenith (New York: Penguin Books, 2001).

3 Finding our true selves

1 The inside flap of Girard's grand opus, *Things Hidden Since the Foundation of the World*, trans. Stephen Bann and Michael Metter (Stanford, CA: Stanford University Press, 1987), offers this synopsis: 'Girard's point of departure is what he calls "mimesis," the conflict that arises when human rivals compete to differentiate themselves from each other, yet succeed only in becoming more and more alike. At certain points in the life of a society, this mimetic conflict erupts into a crisis in which all difference dissolves in indiscriminate violence. In primitive societies, such crises were resolved by the "scapegoating mechanism," in which the community, *en masse*, turns on an unpremeditated victim. The repression of this collective murder and its repetition in ritual sacrifice then forms the foundations of both religion and the restored social order.'

2 See <http://girardianlectionary.net/res/alison_contemplation_violence.htm>. Talk by James Alison, prepared for a day retreat with Sebastian Moore on 'Contemplation in a World of Violence: Girard, Merton, Tolle', Downside Abbey, Bath, 3 November 2001.

4 The art of loss

1 Quoted in Colin Marshall, 'Try Again', *Open Culture*. See <www.openculture.com/2017/12/try-again-fail-again-fail-better-how-samuel-beckett-created-the-unlikely-mantra-that-inspires-entrepreneurs-today.html>.

5 The gifts of the wounded child

1 Hélène Cixous, *Three Steps on the Ladder of Writing* (New York: Columbia University Press, 1993), p. 10.

2 Alice Miller, *The Drama of the Gifted Child* (New York: Basic Books, 1997), from an interview quoted on the back cover.

3 Wayne Muller, *Legacy of the Heart: The Spiritual Advantages of a Painful Childhood* (New York: Fireside, 2002), p. xv.

4 Muller, *Legacy*, p. xiv.

5 Alice Miller, *Prisoners of Childhood* (New York: Basic Books, 1991), p. 85.

6 Fiona Gardner, *The Only Mind Worth Having* (Eugene, OR: Cascade Books, 2015), p. 101.

7 Gardner, *The Only Mind Worth Having*, p. 110.

8 The only written account of this that I know of is in M. Basil Pennington, *Thomas Merton: Brother Monk* (New York: Harper and Row, 1987), p. xii – which is also cited in William H. Shannon's biography, *Silent Lamp: The Thomas Merton Story* (New York: Crossroad, 1992), p. 74.

7 Conversion

1 Paul Wilkes (ed.), *Merton: By Those Who Knew Him Best* (San Francisco, CA: Harper and Row, 1984), p. 115.

2 Wilkes (ed.), *Merton*, p. 110.

8 *My Argument with the Gestapo*

1 John Leonard, 'World War II as a Rorschach Test', *New York Times Book Reviews*, 10 July 1969, p. 35.

2 Mary Gordon, *On Thomas Merton* (Boulder, CO: Shambhala Publications, 2018), p. 68.

9 Escape from escapism

1 Paul Wilkes (ed.), *Merton: By Those Who Knew Him Best* (San Francisco, CA: Harper and Row, 1984), pp. 107–8.

2 Michael Ford, 'Gifts of Gethsemani: Matthew Kelty, Thomas Merton, and the Lessons of Monasticism', *Today's American Catholic*, 15 December 2019.

3 Ron Seitz, *Song for Nobody: A Memory Vision of Thomas Merton* (Liguori, MO: Triumph Books, 1993), pp. 172–3.

10 *The Seven Storey Mountain*

1 Paul Wilkes (ed.), *Merton: By Those Who Knew Him Best* (San Francisco, CA: Harper and Row, 1984), pp. 127–8.

11 What is contemplation?

1 Robert Faricy SJ, 'Merton and Mysticism of the Mind', *The Merton Annual* 11, ed. George Kilcourse (1998). Available at: < http://merton. org/itms/annual/11/Faricy138-147.pdf>.

12 Crossing the Rubicon

1 William H. Shannon, *Silent Lamp: The Thomas Merton Story* (New York: Crossroad, 1992), p. 165.

13 Merton as spiritual director

1 James Finley, *Merton's Palace of Nowhere: A Search for God through Awareness of the True Self* (Notre Dame, IN: Ave Maria Press, 1992 [1978]), p. 111.

15 Apology to an unbeliever

1 Dietrich Bonhoeffer defines cheap grace as 'the preaching of forgiveness without requiring repentance, baptism without church discipline, Communion without confession, absolution without personal confession. Cheap grace is grace without discipleship, grace without the cross, grace without Jesus Christ, living and incarnate.

'Costly grace is the treasure hidden in the field; for the sake of it a man will go and sell all that he has. It is the pearl of great price to buy which the merchant will sell all his goods. It is the kingly rule of Christ, for whose sake a man will pluck out the eye which causes him to stumble; it is the call of Jesus Christ at which the disciple leaves his nets and follows him.' Quoted in *Christianity Today*, 7 February 1994, p. 39.
2 Peter Sloterdijk, *You Must Change Your Life*, trans. Wieland Hoban (Cambridge: Polity Press, 2013), pp. 1–15.
3 See Wayne C. Booth, *Modern Dogma and the Rhetoric of Assent* (Chicago, IL: University of Chicago Press, 1974).
4 From Rainer Maria Rilke's first *Duino Elegy*.

16 'The Root of War is Fear'

1 James Forest, Catholic Worker, in Paul Wilkes (ed.), *Merton: By Those Who Knew Him Best* (San Francisco, CA: Harper and Row, 1984), p. 47.

17 Re-opening the Bible

1 Patrick F. O'Connell, 'Opening the Bible', in *The Thomas Merton Encyclopedia*, ed. William H. Shannon, Christine M. Bochen and Patrick F. O'Connell (Maryknoll, NY: Orbis Books, 2002), p. 342.

2 Ernest Becker, *The Denial of Death* (New York: The Free Press, 1973), p. 91.

3 Michael Cassagram OCSO, 'In Search of a Hidden Wholeness', in *We are Already One*, ed. Gray Henry and Jonathan Montaldo (Louisville, KY: Fons Vitae, 2014), p. 254.

18 Life without care

1 Merton's final talk as novice master (20 August 1965). A recording is also available at <https://soundcloud.com/greg-hillis/thomas-merton-a-life-free-from-care>.

2 Jean Pierre de Caussade, *Abandonment: Or Absolute Surrender to Divine Providence* (Henri Ramiere, Ella MacMahon, 1887), p. 121.

19 The Merton legacy

1 Attributed to Thomas Merton in Ron Seitz's memory vision, *Song for Nobody: A Memory Vision of Thomas Merton* (Liguori, MO: Triumph Books, 1993), pp. 35–6.

2 Paul Wilkes (ed.), *Merton: By Those Who Knew Him Best* (San Francisco, CA: Harper and Row, 1984), p. 111.

3 Slavoj Žižek, *Absolute Recoil* (London: Verso, 2014), pp. 44–5.

4 Žižek, *Absolute Recoil*, p. 45.

5 *IE*, p. 7, cited in James Finley, *Merton's Palace of Nowhere: A Search for God through Awareness of the True Self* (Notre Dame, IN: Ave Maria Press, 1992 [1978]), p. 148.

6 William H. Shannon, *Silent Lamp: The Thomas Merton Story* (New York: Crossroad, 1992), p. 161.

7 Paulo Sorrentino, *The New Pope* (2020). Screenplay available at: <screenplayhttps://tvshowtranscripts.ourboard.org/viewforum.php?f=883>. *The New Pope* is rated MA for mature audiences for mild violence, nudity and adult content.

8 *CGB*, pp. 207–8, quoted by Cassidy Hill in her essay, 'Maybe It's Time for Me to Let Go of Thomas Merton', *Christian Century* (December 2021).

Works cited

Alison, James, 'Contemplation in a World of Violence: Girard, Merton, Tolle', Downside Abbey, Bath, 3 November 2001. Available at: <http://girardianlectionary.net/res/alison_contemplation_violence.htm>.

Aquinas, Thomas, *On the Power of God*, trans. the English Dominican Fathers (Westminster, MD: The Newman Press, 1952).

Arden, M., *Midwifery of the Soul: A Holistic Perspective on Psychoanalysis: Collected Papers of Margaret Arden* (London: Free Association Books, 1998), pp. 4–5.

Arendt, Hannah, *Men in Dark Times* (New York: Harcourt Brace Jovanovich, 1970).

Becker, Ernest, *The Denial of Death* (New York: The Free Press, 1973).

Beckett, Samuel, 'Worstward Ho', quoted in *Books on the Wall* blog. Available at: <https://booksonthewall.com/blog/samuel-beckett-quote-fail-better/>.

Bonhoeffer, Dietrich, 'The Cost of Discipleship, Advent 1937', trans. R. H. Fuller, in *A Testament to Freedom*, ed. Geffrey Kelly and F. Burton Nelson (San Francisco, CA: Harper, 1995 [1990]), pp. 307–21.

Booth, Wayne C., *Modern Dogma and the Rhetoric of Assent* (Chicago, IL: University of Chicago Press, 1974).

Cassagram, Michael, 'In Search of a Hidden Wholeness', in *We are Already One*, ed. Gray Henry and Jonathan Montaldo (Louisville, KY: Fons Vitae, 2014).

Caussade, Jean Pierre de, *Abandonment: Or Absolute Surrender to Divine Providence* (Henri Ramiere, Ella MacMahon, 1887).

Cistercian Quarterly Review 18 (1983).

Cixous, Hélène, *Three Steps on the Ladder of Writing* (New York: Columbia University Press, 1993).

Faricy sj, Robert, 'Merton and Mysticism of the Mind', *The Merton Annual* 11 (1998).

Finley, James, *Merton's Palace of Nowhere: A Search for God through Awareness of the True Self* (Notre Dame, IN: Ave Maria Press, 1992 [1978]).

Ford, Michael, 'Gifts of Gethsemani: Matthew Kelty, Thomas Merton, and the Lessons of Monasticism', *Today's American Catholic*, 15 December 2019.

Gardner, Fiona, *The Only Mind Worth Having* (Eugene, OR: Cascade Books, 2015).

Girard, René, *Things Hidden Since the Foundation of the World*, trans. Stephen Bann and Michael Metter (Stanford, CA: Stanford University Press, 1987 [1978])

Gordon, Mary, *On Thomas Merton* (Boulder, CO: Shambhala Publications, 2018).

Harris, Sam, *The End of Faith* (New York: W. W. Norton, reprint edn, 2005).

Hillis, Greg, 'Thomas Merton: A Life Free from Care' (Soundcloud 2016). Available at: <https://soundcloud.com/greg-hillis/thomas-merton-a-life-free-from-care>.

Kafka, Franz, *The Blue Octavo Notebooks* (Cambridge: Exact Change, llustrated edn, 2004).

Kierkegaard, Søren, *The Present Age*, trans. Alexander Dru (San Francisco, CA: Harper and Row, 1962), p. 105.

Leonard, John, 'World War II as a Rorschach Test', *New York Times Book Reviews*, 10 July 1969.

Marshall, Colin, 'Try Again', *Open Culture*. Available at: <www.openculture.com/2017/12/try-again-fail-again-fail-better-how-samuel-beckett-created-the-unlikely-mantra-that-inspires-entrepreneurs-today.html>.

Maugham, Somerset, *Of Human Bondage* (CreateSpace Independent Publishing Platform, 2018).

Merton, Thomas, *The Asian Journal of Thomas Merton*, ed. Naomi Burton, Brother Patrick Hart and James Laughlin (New York:

New Directions, 1975).

Merton, Thomas, *The Climate of Monastic Prayer* (Kalamazoo, MI: Cistercian Publications, 1969).

Merton, Thomas, *Conjectures of a Guilty Bystander* (Garden City, NY: Doubleday, 1966).

Merton, Thomas, *Contemplation in a World of Action* (Garden City, NY: Doubleday, 1971).

Merton, Thomas, *Contemplative Prayer* (Garden City, NY: Doubleday, 1971).

Merton, Thomas, *The Courage for Truth*, ed. Christine M. Bochen (New York: Farrar, Straus and Giroux, 1993).

Merton, Thomas, *Disputed Questions* (New York: Harcourt Brace Jovanovich, 1960).

Merton, Thomas, *Faith and Violence: Christian Teaching and Christian Practice*, Notre Dame, IN: University of Notre Dame Press, 1968).

Merton, Thomas, *The Hidden Ground of Love: Letters on Religious Experience and Social Concerns*, ed. William H. Shannon (New York: Harcourt Brace Jovanovich, 1985).

Merton, Thomas, *Honorable Reader: Reflections on My Work*, ed. Robert Daggy (New York: Crossroad, 1989).

Merton, Thomas, *The Inner Experience: Notes on Contemplation*, ed. William H. Shannon (San Francisco, CA: HarperSanFrancisco, 2003).

Merton, Thomas, *The Literary Essays of Thomas Merton*, ed. Patrick Hart (New York: New Directions, 1981).

Merton, Thomas, *Living Bread* (New York: Farrar, Straus and Giroux, 1980 [1956]).

Merton, Thomas, *Love and Living*, ed. Naomi Burton Stone and Brother Patrick Hart (New York: Farrar, Straus and Giroux, 1979 [1975]).

Merton, Thomas, *My Argument with the Gestapo* (Garden City, NY: Doubleday, 1969).

Merton, Thomas, *New Seeds of Contemplation* (New York: New Directions, 1972 [1961]).

Merton, Thomas, *No Man is an Island* (New York: Harcourt Brace Jovanovich, 1983 [1955]).

Merton, Thomas, *Opening the Bible* (Collegeville, MN: Liturgical Press, 1970).

Merton, Thomas, *The Pocket Thomas Merton*, ed. Robert Inchausti (Boulder, CO: Shambhala Publications, 2005).

Merton, Thomas, *Raids on the Unspeakable* (New York: New Directions, 1966).

Merton, Thomas, *The School of Charity: Letters of Thomas Merton on Religious Renewal and Spiritual Direction*, ed. Brother Patrick Hart (New York: Farrar, Straus and Giroux, 1990).

Merton, Thomas, *A Search for Solitude: Pursuing the Monk's True Life, The Journals of Thomas Merton*, vol. 3: 1952–1960 (San Francisco, CA: HarperOne, 1997).

Merton, Thomas, *The Secular Journal of Thomas Merton* (New York: Farrar, Straus and Cudahy, 1959).

Merton, Thomas, *Seeds of Destruction* (New York: Farrar, Straus and Giroux, 1964).

Merton, Thomas, *The Seven Storey Mountain* (San Diego, CA: Harcourt Brace Jovanovich, 1998 [1948]).

Merton, Thomas, *The Sign of Jonas* (New York: Harcourt Brace Jovanovich, 1953).

Merton, Thomas, *Thomas Merton: A Life in Letters; The Essential Collection*, ed. William H. Shannon and Christine M. Bochen (New York: HarperCollins, 2008).

Merton, Thomas, *A Thomas Merton Reader*, ed. Thomas P. McDonnell (New York: Doubleday, 1974).

Merton, Thomas, *Thoughts in Solitude* (New York: Farrar, Straus and Giroux, 1956, 1958).

Merton, Thomas, 'Time and Liturgy', *Worship* 31 (December 1956), pp. 2–10.

Merton, Thomas, *Wisdom of the Desert* (New York: New Directions, 1961).

Merton, Thomas, *Zen and the Birds of Appetite* (New York: New Directions, 1968).

Merton, Thomas, with Robert Daggy, *Road to Joy: Letters to New and Old Friends* (New York: Farrar, Straus and Giroux, 1989).

Miller, Alice, *The Drama of the Gifted Child* (New York: Basic Books, 1997).

Miller, Alice, *Prisoners of Childhood* (New York: Basic Books, 1991 [1981]).

Muller, Wayne, *Legacy of the Heart: The Spiritual Advantages of a Painful Childhood* (New York: Fireside, 2002).

O'Connell, Patrick F., 'Opening the Bible', in *The Thomas Merton Encyclopedia*, ed. William H. Shannon, Christine M. Bochen and Patrick F. O'Connell (Maryknoll, NY: Orbis Books, 2002).

O'Donoghue, John, *Eternal Echoes: Reflections on Our Yearning to Belong* (New York: HarperCollins, 1999).

Pennington, M. Basil, *Thomas Merton: Brother Monk* (New York: Harper and Row, 1987).

Pessoa, Fernando, *The Book of Disquiet*, ed. and trans. Richard Zenith (New York: Penguin Books, 2001).

Rohr, Richard, *Immortal Diamond* (San Francisco, CA: Jossey Bass, 2013).

Seitz, Ron, *Song for Nobody: A Memory Vision of Thomas Merton* (Liguori, MO: Triumph Books, 1993).

Shannon, William H., *Silent Lamp: The Thomas Merton Story* (New York: Crossroad, 1992).

Sloterdijk, Peter, *You Must Change Your Life*, trans. Wieland Hoban (Cambridge: Polity Press, 2013).

Sorrentino, Paolo, *The New Pope* (2020). Screenplay available at: <screenplayhttps://tvshowtranscripts.ourboard.org/viewforum.php?f=883>.

Wilkes, Paul (ed.), *Merton: By Those Who Knew Him Best* (San Francisco, CA: Harper and Row, 1984).

Williams, Rowan, *A Silent Action: Engagements with Thomas Merton* (Louisville, KY: Fons Vitae, 2011).

Wordsworth, William, 'Ode: Intimations of Immortality from Recollections in Early Childhood', in *English Romantic Poetry*, ed. Stanley Appelbaum (Mineola, NY: Dover Publications, 1996).

Žižek, Slavoj, *Absolute Recoil* (London: Verso, 2014).